BENEATH THE SURFACE

LAVANYA MATHUR

BookLeaf Publishing
India | USA | UK

Presentation by *BookLeaf Publishing*

Web: www.bookleafpub.com

E-mail: info@bookleafpub.com

ISBN: 9789367398524

First edition 2025

This is for everyone who inspired me in some shape or form. Special thanks to my parents

CONTENTS

Poem

THE LONG JOURNEY

Part of a mourning dove I was,
She flapped her wings,
Forsake me in no time,
I'm useless now, I thought,
Coming to an end is all I've got

Flowing with the winds,
Searching ways to end,
Landed on a balcony,
Saw a man hitting his wife,
Pointless I felt, couldn't save her life,
Nothing she said, like it's her fate,
'Stop!' I protested, he didn't listen,
Finally, the son came rushing, finding courage,
Thank God! I sighed in relief,
'Stop or I'll kill you,' he said trembling,
Going to slap his child, retaliating,
That mother stopped him and stood for herself,
She found courage,

I Flew

Sat on a tree,
Looking into a window—a happy couple,
Some love, some hope I see,
Phone rang, he was frightened,
Asked her to shush,
Picked and said, 'I'll pick Sandra from school,
Will be back for our anniversary soon,'
'I love you,' she said like she meant it,
He hung up,
I love you, said his regret
He cried,

I Flew

After an hour,
Resting on a slab,
Looking towards a lady, all sweaty and pale,
Is this a rat kill I see!
She put a few drops in the tea,
Saw someone coming,
An old lady I see, 'You are not my daughter-in-law
But a daughter to me,' she said
'I'm sorry, is this tea for me?'
'No, it's stale,' she replied immediately
They hugged,

I Flew

Finally reached a hostel I suppose,
A teenager caught my eye,
Happy in a strange way, I observed every action he made,

Ready and suited up as if going on a date,
Looking towards a letter—*Love letter,* said my poor judgement,
Things changed unexpectedly,
He took a rope, 'I'm lonely,' said the wall,
Just when about to hang, his parents arrived,
Happy Birthday! They exclaimed,
He stopped,

I Flew

It's a long journey today,
I am just a feather,
Can life be so ugly? That's all I could gather,
A huge lake, my chance to drown,
To finish my existence,
Why can't I do it now?
What changed my mind?
Part of a dreamcatcher I am now,
With some friends and an existence that counts,
Often wonder what stopped me,
HOPE, that it will be fine,
The wind whispered.

–Iris

SHE

Between the chaos of this world,
Misunderstood, shattered, and confused
Going far away from herself, connecting the dots that made no sense

Falling into a deep blue sea,
Breaking, waking, breaking with no hope,
No trust she sees,
Just empty roads with nowhere to go,
They called her a troubled child,
Indeed! She was a black sheep,

Time taught her what she can be,
Endless nights of crying to sleep,
Empty conversations,
Questioning her identity, her beliefs
There came her god,
Concluding her despondency.

He developed like a fragrance she loved,
In the people she met, the places she visited, in her every thought.

Breathing a bit deeper with every breath she took,
She heard her voice far away,
Shouting at the top of her lungs,
She is her counselor, she is a warrior,
A new chapter of her life has begun.

All questions became her answers,
All sorrows shaped perspective,
Seeing the world in a different light,
She attracted people alike.

She is the writer of her dreams,
Looking back with a smile on her face,
Because in the darkest of rooms,
There was faith.

– Iris

I WISH

I wish I were a bird,
Independent as I can be

I wish I were a bird,
Reckless and free

I wish I were a bird,
Singing songs upbeat

I wish I were a bird,
Not caring about despondency

I wish I were a bird,
Content with my being

I wish I were a bird,
Seizing the moment as I please

I wish I were a bird,
Visiting places I want to be

I wish I were a bird,
Trusting my wings to carry me

I wish I were a bird,
Living in the moment,
Cheerful with full energy

I wish I were a bird,
Flying through the weightless clouds,
Drifting like a fulfilled vitality

I wish I were a bird,
Discontinuing things affecting peace

I wish I were a bird,
Untroubled with who stays, who leaves

I wish I were a bird,
Breathing through the fresh breeze

I wish I were a bird,
With no attachments, no regrets, no grief
I wish I were a bird,
If,
I never followed my dreams.

A FRIEND

A friend he was when he came into my life,
It was weird how we never talked in life,
Talking to him was never a task,
It was like we knew each other for ages; we hit it off over anything you could ask.

Meeting him felt like the calm of when the sun hits the dusk,
He felt at home in a city entirely of chaos,
He became the best part of my day, giving my story a different tangent,
It was effortless,
It was the best thing you could imagine.

It never required time,
Even ten minutes of conversation was enough to instill peace in my mind,
It was slow .. it was written that way,
We all deserve this friendship, I will pray

It took a hundred hurdles to stand upright,
Knowing what is wrong and what is right,
Nevertheless, it was meant to be that way,
'Maktub,' as they call it,
it was destiny, as they say,

Some people go, some people stay,
He taught me what I want from myself, what I can do, and what I will do today,

He knew what I wanted, what I was thinking, even when I didn't utter a word,
I lived a bit more than I ever did with a friend who made me love myself.

There are ties we let go of, and there are bonds that stay,
In all the uncertainties, one thing I am sure of still,
I have a bond to look up to,
a tale to tell.

A SMELL

A newborn she was, her mother's lap gave her peace,
holding her father's finger put her at ease
Oh then, the Golden days of childhood arrived,
Sandy aroma of that playground touched her heart,
excited her mind,
Living through life she neglects those smells,
What they say, what they can tell

That growing time of her life transpired,
Happy as a day, full of life and inspired,
At school, the smell of lunch boxes and cheerful
classrooms was her relief,
Sensing people around her, it was a fun place to be,
Living through life she neglects those smells,
What they say, what they can tell

Somewhat she grew,
A little after fifteen and a little before twenty-two,
She didn't particularly fit in, neither did she want to
The smell of her books and her company gave peace,
A friend she got as she got older
The smell of her dog was all over her coat,
Living through life she neglects those smells,
What they say, what they can tell

The earthy smell of rain offered content
And one day,
It all makes sense,
What felt comforting and what you resist,
When the sun looks brighter, the days are beautiful, and someone more important than your being,
How did it happen, she thought to herself,
She went back to those days, a nostalgia she felt,
What smells she neglected,
what they say, what they told

Because
Reading her vows,
Today she knows,
He smells like home,
Her home!

THE MUSIC

A little boy,
Maybe eight or nine,
Walking by that lane to school
Usual like every day,
Content, at peace
Happy and gay

Disturbing traffic lights, distracting people,
Growing at an unusual pace,
He was that kid who got observant by age,
Thinking he'd get what he chooses, see what he sees,
He chooses to sing, dance, ignore, and rejoice in his own melody

Loo became winds in no time,
Observing everything around him,
Trees whispering like wind chimes,
So much noise he thought,
But so much peace at the same time,
Like the music of being present around him,
Got into his heart, into his mind

A little further on that road,
Blue and green beauty,
Excited, he exclaimed, 'A peacock!',
Fascinated by every move it made,
So much noise he thought,
But so much peace at the same time,
Like the music of being present around him,
Got into his heart, into his mind
Nature is a giver, he knew,
Creating what his dreams won't get through,
A dancing peacock singing, calling out the rains from the sky above,
A cool breeze kissed his cheeks,
It was a pleasant afternoon,
Extraordinary how a sunny march became a pre-monsoon shower in June,
So much noise, he thought,
But so much peace at the same time,
Like the music of being present around him,
Got into his heart, into his mind

Tip-tip, tap-tap, happy droplets everywhere,
Deserted land flourished again,
Every breeze calming his senses,
The smell of wet mud and cooling winds,
Looking up, feeling every drop of rain rushing down,
So much noise, he thought,
But so much peace at the same time,
Like the music of being present around him,
Got into his heart, into his mind
A brief shower it was,
Enough to put the surroundings on pause,
Laughing greenery, now greener,

Dusty air now cleaner,
Hidden animals now playing their songs,
So much noise, he thought,
But so much peace at the same time,
Like the music of being present around him,
Got into his heart, into his mind

Finally, in front of the gates,
Content in an unusual way,
Recalling his journey on the way to school,
Like he understood what to see and what not to,
The noisy roads don't feel noisy anymore,
He saw what he had never seen before,
It's all a game of putting presence and time,
Where we keep our thoughts and depths of the mind,
So much noise, he thought,
But so much peace at the same time,
Like the music of being present around him,
Got into his heart, into his mind

–Iris

Stories

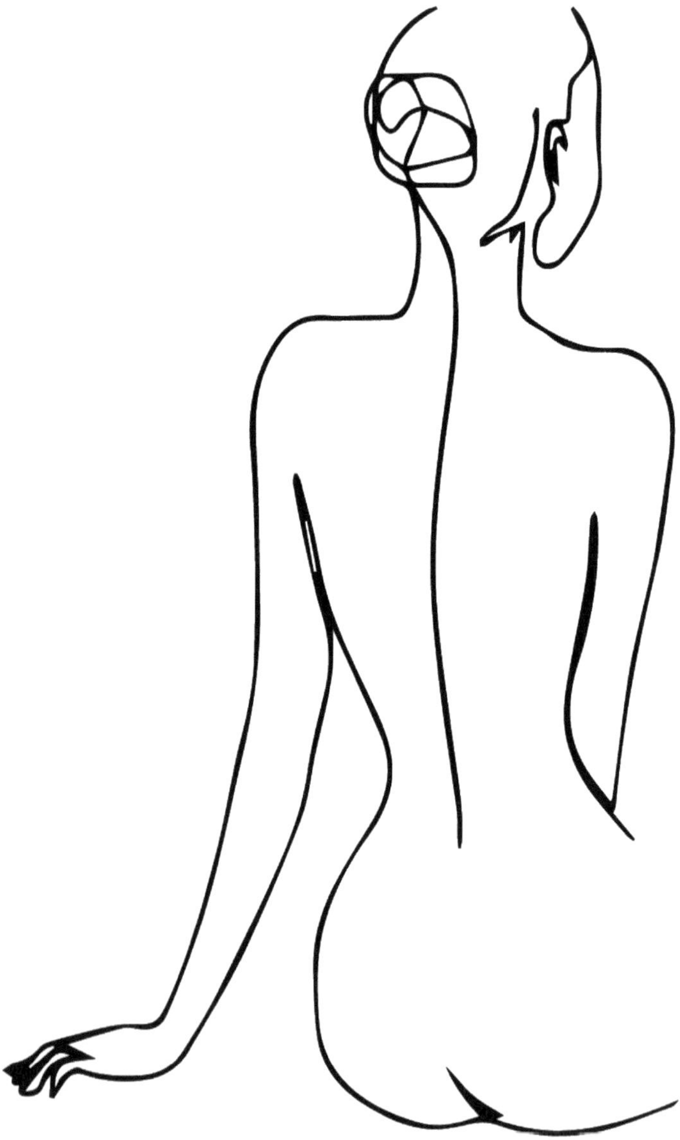

ONE LAST TIME

In a beautiful, warm, and welcoming town in Switzerland, the sun shone brighter, nights felt calmer, and the snow was the most beautiful thing you could ever see. The people, along with its mesmerizing scenic beauty, made the town what it was. The town wasn't the fanciest, but it still had everything needed to maintain internal peace. The city sang beautiful stories of friendships, relationships, and bonds that never broke, creating a magical aura that entices every tourist to visit the town and experience all that it offers.

Hey there, it's Iris,

I want to share one of the stories from that town in Switzerland. It is a tale of friendship between two girls, Mickey and Diana.

Let's get to know Mickey first. A young, enthusiastic girl with dreams as big as the ocean, you will often find her daydreaming. She saw the world differently, and that was her beauty. She was new in town. A younger sibling, reckless and unrestrained. Freedom made her happy, and even a cold rain shower thrilled her.

Mickey and Diana were neighbours, but they hardly met each other and were nothing but acquaintances for a long time. They usually met in town gatherings, exchanging only a few words. Yet, every time they looked at each other, they smiled—and it was always genuine.

A year passed, and on one tranquil Sunday evening, Diana decided to take her dog JoJo on a walk. JoJo was Diana's baby, her most precious being on this planet.

Oh, I just remembered that I had to tell you about Diana. So, Diana…She was a lovely, pleasant, and genuine girl, a nurturer by her very nature. She always knew how to give and never expected anything in return. She felt too profoundly and got hurt too quickly, but that was simply who she was. She tried to change but just couldn't. Now, she's found peace and happiness in embracing who she was and whatever she felt. It gave her purpose—a purpose that went beyond herself. The sunset felt warmer that day as she walked with JoJo.

It was a typical day until JoJo decided to run towards that wide main road that connected the city with the country's capital. Diana couldn't stop JoJo and was screaming at the top of her lungs, watching a truck speeding close. It was too far for JoJo to notice or hear the sound in time. Mickey was on the other side, saw she was closer and realized she could still make it before Diana. JoJo was a toy pom, which was hardly noticeable from the truck driver's view. Whatever it was, the main concern was that someone needed to save JoJo. Mickey decided to jump in so the driver would stop. She waved her hands toward the driver as he continued driving at full speed, risking her life for that little thing.

It worked! The truck driver stopped within inches of them. Mickey took a big sigh of relief and looked towards Diana.

Diana looked at her in tears, smiling, and ran to hug her. "It's okay," said Mickey. They held each other.

And always stayed.

Since that day, their friendship grew and became stronger. They started doing everything together, and slowly, with time, their relationship aged into a precious bond. They said you can find a soul mate in a sister from another mother, and both knew they believed in it. It was a kind of friendship where they knew what the other wanted without telling each other, felt each other's pain, and were always genuinely happy for each other. It is a rare thing to find in today's world—something to cherish, something to keep.

July 19th was Mickey's birthday, and before the birthday party, like always, they decided to spend time together before arriving at the gathering. Standing by the silent lake near the town, the girls gazed at the night sky full of enchanting stars that twinkled innocently, creating a beautiful pattern. "I want to be one of the stars," said Mickey. "We would be one day," Diana assured, promising they would go to a big city together someday. All they need to do is work hard enough.

Being from a small town, they were not born with any privileges. They had to make their own destiny, and they were ready to do that. They understood that only they could change their reality and were ready to put in the work. Together.

Like always.

They worked hard to save enough money, doing multiple odd jobs daily while finding time to study for the entrance exams. They got into a good college that could be a portal to their new life in the city. And finally, they stood together in front of the same lake with an offer letter. This time, they felt like stars brighter than the daylight.

There was just one problem: they got different locations.

"It will never be a problem, love," said Diana. "Of course, we got each other," said Mickey.

With a vision in their eyes, they were delighted that they would finally live their dream and get everything they wanted.

It was comforting to know that they had each other's support throughout this journey; it gave them a sense of calm and assurance. And even though they couldn't meet each other daily, they had a time set for a video call every day. Just knowing they had each other was enough, and indeed, it was.

Every second Saturday, they set a coffee ritual—an unsaid promise to meet each other and sit at the same table on the rooftop at 6 p.m. Together, they'd watch the sun gently kiss the horizon and release mesmerizing colors, painting the sky pink, green, yellow, and orange simultaneously. Somewhere near the golden hour, the sky opened its heart to the approaching night. Just like they used to, this time, in front of the city of their dreams.

You know how life becomes when you finally join the rat race, right?

Complex emotions peak, and you realize more about yourself than ever. You unlearn so much about what you thought was the reality, and you finally realize that there is no one for you but yourself. Yet, amidst all this, life becomes so much easier when you have that one person you can call an exception. Your soul mate is a friend who helps you through all hardships—smiling, laughing, and making life worthwhile, effortlessly giving the championship we all crave.

Those few hours in the Rose Café were enough to keep them sane. They both waited to get through the hectic week and finally met for some quality time.

Time played its game as it always does, and eventually, these dates started getting cancelled because Mickey became so busy that even the calls went unanswered. Diana, her good friend, understood every time and hoped that Mickey would come and meet her soon to laugh, rant, and cry again. She missed hearing stories of that hot guy in the neighbourhood, sharing never-ending office gossip, or talking about how much she misses her parents back home.

Around mid-September that year, Diana sent a heartfelt voice note to her friend Mickey, telling her how much she missed her. She looked at the sunset that day with a sinking feeling in her heart and tears in her eyes. Maybe this one meant more than any other in the line, but just like all her other voicemails, this one found its way into the queue just like that.

Waiting to be heard. Heard soon.

Mickey was out of town for a two-week business trip; she never bothered to hear the messages. Being the reckless one, she didn't think much of it and decided to listen to them when she was home. But she got busy again and completely forgot.

Gazing at the beautiful sky from an open window in her kitchen, Mickey got some time to relax. She finally went through her voicemails six months after returning,

Hey Mick, it is me!

Mickey felt a rush of emotions inside her, almost like she was about to break down in tears, craving that one hug from her friend. *I have been so lost in the hustle*, screamed the tears rolling down her eyes.

She listened to Diana's voicemail and realized how much she missed her friend—laughing with her and hearing the funny stories of her life.

Ahh, what happened to me? Mickey thought to herself and called her friend Diana right away.

It was a man. "What's your name, dear?"

"It's Mickey. Who am I talking to? I have called Diana."

"Mickey?" asked the man.

"Yes, it is me. Who is this?" Mickey questioned, surprised.

"I am Diana's neighbor," a deep, aged voice replied. "I am sorry to tell you this, but we lost her last week. She was strong and tried her best to survive, but there was too much bleeding."

Mickey felt as though someone had thrown a massive rock at her heart. "Oh shit, I can't breathe," responded Mickey.

"Sit anywhere near you and try to take deep breaths," said the man with concern in his voice.

She grabbed a chair by the table and gently sat, holding her head in despair, absorbing what she had just heard or at least tried to.

"What do you mean by operation? What happened to her? Diana, if that's a prank, then it is not funny," she said in disbelief.

"She had an accident, and the doctors tried to get her through it for the first two days, but the injuries were too severe, and we lost her. I am sorry. She tried her best to survive. She was a warrior."

"What do you mean, *was*. Huh? What is happening? Is this real?"

The man suggested she rest and not go out for the day, and call him at his number in case she needed something. He courteously gave her his number, telling her it would take time but everything would be okay.

The sun was setting, and Mickey sat on the chair looking towards the sky from the glass door that opened to her balcony. It has always been the sunsets, Diana, but today, there is no color in the sky. There never will be. She thought to herself.

The realization that the last time they met was truly their final meeting haunted her, teaching her a painful lesson in the hardest way possible.

She started thinking of the day they'd last met, trying to recall every single detail—what she wore, what she said, and even what she'd ordered.

A picture, yes, there is a picture.

They took a picture together that day. When she opened her gallery to see the picture, tears welled up in her eyes. She poured her heart out, feeling terrible for not knowing about her death and for not being a good friend.

She thought about the people she loves and cares for, and the possibility of losing them one day.

That day, she decided to meet all of them again as if she were meeting them for the last time.

Starting from everyone back home to the cleaning lady in her office. She hugged them so tight, telling them they meant something to her. Completely present in each moment, taking pictures with them so as to capture the memory and hold onto them forever.

Appreciating and being grateful for everyone in her life.

After meeting everybody that Saturday evening, she dressed up to go to the café.

She sat at the same table, smiling looking at the pictures of her loved ones whom she had met over this time. Recalling all the bitter and sweet memories with them.

The last photo was of her and Diana. She was admiring that picture just when the two cups of coffee that had been ordered arrived.

Taking a sip, she watched the sun go down with Diana for one last time.

A PENGUIN OF THE CAGE

Hey there, it's Iris,

Once, there was a penguin called Novel. He lived in a zoo park where thousands of people visited him. Everyone loved his tricks and called him the "king penguin." Many people especially came to the Zoo just to see this unique penguin. The other penguins were highly jealous of him, and they often wondered what he had that they lacked and why they did not have a fan following like him. However, Novel used to work extra hard to be on stage, pushing himself to the point of exhaustion every day. He missed having a normal everyday life and often wondered why he had no friends and time to relax like other penguins in the Zoo. He was very envious of the comfortable life that the other penguins seemed to have.

One day, Novel had the privilege of joining penguins from the ice mountain nearby, who lived in a natural habitat, for a show. He couldn't help but feel jealous of all the penguins who lived in the wild and got to experience freedom and everyday life which every penguin deserved. *Why am I caged in this Zoo?* He thought to himself. *I wish I could escape.*

Among the many penguins of the ice land was a female named Carla! Carla was a natural in the wild. After being released from the zoo, she had adapted well to her new life, enjoying the snow and playing freely. She felt lucky to live like an ordinary penguin. That's what Novel thought.

However, after her release from the Zoo, she missed home and her friends so much. Having been part of that protected environment since birth, it was difficult for her to adjust to life without humans, surrounded only by other animals—some of whom wanted to be her friend, while others who never wanted good for her. She was still adjusting, and finding food became a constant struggle. As she watched Novel from the Zoo and how he could return to his safe space after his act made Carla envious of him.

They envy each other for reasons that do not exist, thinking the other lives a dream life.

This story is a short example of how we function in ordinary life. Yet, at a glance, it seems crazy how unsatisfied we can be with all we have and how envious we become of what others have. How we long for what is not ours, while completely neglecting that what we do might be what someone longs for today.

In my opinion, constant complaining and anxiety about things we don't have or have no control over corrupt the experiences our reality is willing to offer. It is almost too late to realize when we get wholly invested in this loop; a loop that never ends but intensifies with time.

If Novel had taken the time to appreciate his popularity, talent, and the safety of his protected environment in which he lived, he wouldn't have been unsatisfied with what he had. He would have never felt the absence of what he thought was missing in his life.

Being satisfied doesn't mean settling for what you have and not longing for more, but it means being happy with the result of all the efforts you have made so far and being confident that something great is always in store for you like it is right now, at this very moment.

We don't realize how often we disturb our mental peace by obsessing over what we don't have, not knowing we will be happy when we finally have it.

Trust me, just realizing this and living a simple life is the solution to many problems. All you need to do is stop running in the race and start being your person with a life unaffected by others. It is hard sometimes when all you want is a long catch. And then, you see everyone getting what they have always longed for. Still, if you appreciate your life's uniqueness and experiences, knowing they are made just for you because only you can live through them with grace and lessons to take, you will receive faster than you would have imagined. It's all about the energies you release subconsciously, which get back to you in the form of blessings.

Someone else's life might look good to you today, and you might wish to have that girl's hair, or that car, or that person's family. However, when you look closely, you'll realize you are exactly where you should be, doing exactly what you should. There is no point in covetousness, because what makes living beautiful is that each of us have different stories and journeys, which makes this world one big story we call *life*.

Therefore, never undermine where you live because what you see from afar looks like what everyone would love to get. You never know they might be looking right back at you, wishing to find an address on your street. Because right here is the only place you are supposed to be.

UNCONSCIOUSLY SUBCONSCIOUS

It was a summer evening; Martha and Alia, two best friends, had the best summer break.

They used to do everything together; both the girls were into football, so they decided to join the club, and it was the best decision they could have made. It was a two-month camp with a district-level tournament for all the teams at the end. The best part was that if they got selected, they would represent their city and end up in the Nationals.

Little did they know that things were about to change unexpectedly.

After a month of hard training, the finals were almost near. Both the girls were riding their bicycles on the usual route.

Suddenly, a truck approached them at a strange speed; the driver, anxious and hasty, shouted that the brakes had failed, but the lane was extremely narrow. The girls hardly had only a few seconds to react. They managed to get to the farthest corner of the road so as to avoid getting hit by the truck, but their legs were caught under the tires.

Martha's left leg was injured miserably, and Alia's right leg stopped responding after the accident. A man passing by took them to a nearby hospital. When they opened their eyes, they had plastered all over their feet.

Hey there, it's Iris,

We often find ourselves in situations where there seems to be no escape. We curse the universe for letting it happen and accept it as our fate. There are multiple instances where we find ourselves trapped or lost due to occurrences beyond our control.

These things don't have to be big or small; unknowingly, we encounter multiple instances of being caught. It is easy to allow the negative energies around us to facilitate our inner system during such times, but it is often never the answer.

Doing so only magnifies our pain and makes it worse than it needs to be, which is not a desirable outcome. Instead, the question is: what can be done?

After the operation, Martha and Alia were devastated by their fate. The girls struggled to understand what had happened to them and what lay ahead. It is never easy to think of what has happened, accept it, and move on. It took much courage to get to the point where they were.

Martha used to cry and mourn, lying down on the bed next to Alia, knowing that she wouldn't be able to walk for another three months.

On the other hand, Alia started reading books on spiritual healing and affirmations. It changed her mind and thought process. She used to say, "I am exactly where I am supposed to be."

For Alia, there seemed to be no reason to mourn or feel remorse about the incident.

Martha was surprised at Alia's mindset and thought that her friend had gone mad after the incident, so she started spouting these weird theories.

But whenever Martha said anything, Alia kept quiet and listened, without interrupting and disregarding anything, because only she could feel its positive changes on her.

Eventually, both the girls were trained to move their legs. But Martha always said, "What will ever happen in these three weeks? I will have to live with this. It is such a waste of time."

On the other hand, Alia promised to strengthen herself and become stronger, which she eventually did. For example, she used affirmations like, "I am not weak; this is just a small injury; I will heal in no time and make it to the game."

Despite her condition being more severe than Martha's, Alia made far more progress. Everyone in the hospital was surprised and called it a miracle, though the miracle was inside her heart, in the deepest part of her consciousness. Alia learned the art of tricking her subconscious mind unconsciously.

First, she used affirmations by will and tricked her cautious mind into it. Then, once that was achieved, her unconscious mind started inculcating positive affirmations inside her head.

That's exactly how we train our minds to always stay positive—fake it till you make it, as they say.

Of course, as per critics, being optimistic about everything is simply straying far away from reality, but the truth is, we humans underestimate the power of our subconscious minds.

We are a product of what we feed to our subconscious minds unconsciously, and that is precisely why some people stay determined to their goals and achieve them while others take a U-turn when faced with an obstacle along the way.

Determination and persistence, along with a strong attitude, are fundamentals for staying consistent while achieving positivity through affirmations.

The road is never easy, and distractions are a part of the journey, but when you know what you want, then it becomes easier to overcome all hurdles—whether negative people or testing situations—because your brain recognizes that it is affecting your purpose.

It's funny how we spend so much time worrying about what we think through our conscious minds, yet we ignore the great force that drives it all. Experts say that the subconscious mind can be up to a million times more powerful than the conscious mind.

We hear things like, "Dream of the stars, and you'll reach the moon," or "Believe, and it will happen." We tend to take such lines as motivational quotes, and completely overlook the reason why they are motivational quotes.

As a person, I have experienced its magic over my life when things have hit rock bottom, and so I advocate this technique for you to become the master of your own life and your fate because ultimately, it's no one but *you* who decides it. Just like Alia and Martha did, as a result, at 10 a.m. on match day, Alia played and won the football game with her incredible team, while Martha was getting ready for her next physiotherapy session with the same mindset as before.

Our subconscious is the source of our beliefs and limitations quite literally. They limit us from achieving success in any sphere of life and attaining happiness. Our naïve brain takes these limiting thoughts as facts, and our subconscious accepts them, applying them to our daily lives—when they are only a part of our imagination. Eventually, we lose grip of our lives, and our limiting beliefs become our ground reality.

So now, when your past or future limits your being,
Come to the present, have faith
And tell yourself, "I believe."

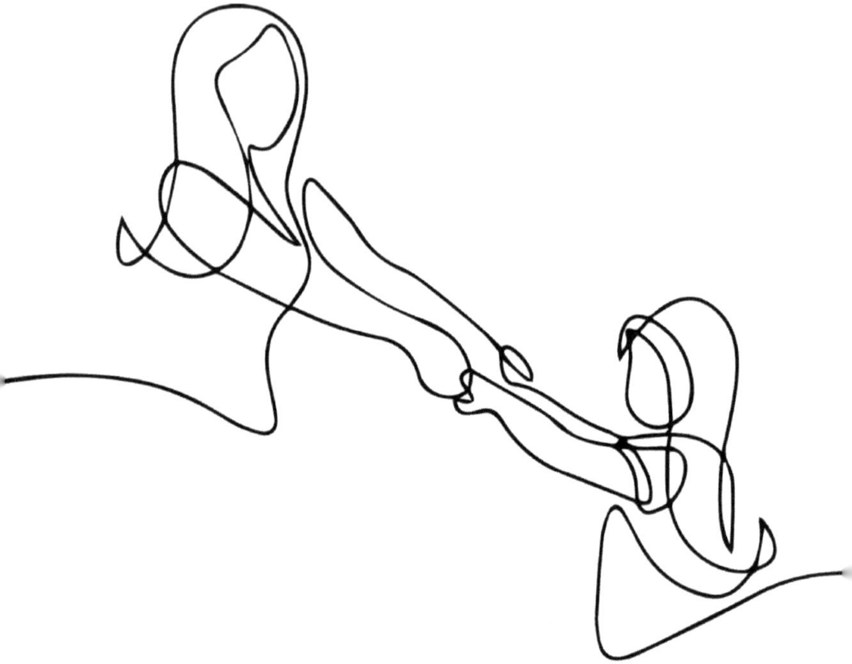

I LOVE YOU

This is about a mother's love, the purest form of love there ever can be.

The kind of love that can take you back to your childhood, even when you have passed your 40s; the love that reminds you of the earthy smell of rain, the love as comforting as the smell of marshmallows, and the warmth of rusty smoke on a cold winter night.

It's incredible how I can go on and on with these examples, but they would never be enough. So now I leave the comfort of your mother's affection to your symbolic representation.

Hey there, it's Iris,

This one is about a mother's love.

The bond is an emotion in itself.

Not to sound overly dramatic, but it's the only thing you will ever need in your life.

My relationship with my mother has been sweet and savory, mixed with a few spices here and there.

Regardless, the warmth remains despite whatever happens. You love your mother, and she loves you back every day in her unique ways.

Some, you will understand, while some, you won't.

Nonetheless, she will always look at you with a smile whenever you come home, waiting for you to have that meal she can't have without you.

This is a story about the time I got severely sick and was home for treatment; the tenure taught me many things, and I was and still am grateful for all I learned during that time.

Little did I know a significant lesson was yet to knock on my doorstep, one that I am now sharing. I hope it will help you appreciate or relive life's greatest blessing.

After one of the longest days of my life, I hoped to get fit enough to go check my blood test results to see my dog and feel the satisfaction of home.

I remember the day I was back; I wanted to treat myself with a kinder joy because I heard this chocolate tasted terrific, and there was a toy inside—a little girl in armor.

I did not think much of it; it kept falling on the dining table where it was kept on for the entire duration until I fully recovered. I was waiting to recover and return to my university in another city.

Two months later, I was home for vacation, and while dusting the shelves, I saw that girl on the rack standing tall as ever.

I stood there looking at it for a while, getting teary-eyed—not only because the girl is now strong but more importantly, because it was my mother's love, so she had decorated that little plastic doll with beautiful antique pieces on her shelf.

It may seem like a minor incident, but it was a reminder that there was and will always be an expression of love in her every action.

This kind of love is rare to find; paradoxically, it is always with you, just at home.

I still don't understand a lot of things she says or does, but you know what?

Just like me,
Now, go back home without needing to understand her,
Just kiss her cheek, hug her tight, and say, "I love you," because that's what she has been waiting to hear all her life.

I love you, Mom.

THE SCREEN PLAY

Samantha has lived in Boston all her life; she was raised like an average kid in her area.

Her mother and father loved and protected her as any parent would. They always kept her safe in a little cocoon, where she was comforted and shielded from harsh realities of life. She spent 18 years of her life like that, totally unaware of what's next to come.

Finally, she enrolled in the college of her dreams, and it was time for her to leave; moving to New York City, away from her parents for the first time, marked a huge shift in her life.

She struggled to cope and faced multiple backlashes along the way; she was still figuring out how to navigate this world—whom to trust and whom not to? How to react and when not to? What can something mean, and why are people the way they are?

All these doubts, confusions, and questions affected her mental health to the extent that she felt she wasn't ready for this world.

The only question which plagued her was: Why are people the way they are, and why can't they be the way she wants them to be?

Hey there, it's Iris,

Most of you could relate to Samantha's story; some of you might be going through this process, while some might have already moved past it.

Regardless, at some point in our lives, we all face situations where we encounter certain people or life circumstances—where we feel the need to put on a face for the world while a rush of emotions run deep inside—which no one else sees but you.

I moved past this phase after numerous experiences and lessons, becoming almost mechanical to survive it.

Somehow, my answer is slightly different from what you might expect. So here I am, sharing it in hopes that it might help you—today, tomorrow, or whenever you read this.

When I was fed up with my situation on various fronts, it made me question the reality of everything. True to the saying, "God helps you when you want to be helped," I came across a quote by the famous American screenwriter and novelist Charlie Kaufman: "*Everything I've written is personal; it's the only way I know how to write.*"

Just as Charlie writes movies about his life, our lives are like a screenplay.

Think about it: from being born in Boston to making her way to New York City, to ultimately reaching a point where Samantha begins questioning life and embarks on a quest to find the answer. How can it be a mere coincidence or even her choice? When we look at all the past events standing far away, all under one umbrella, it becomes easier to accept that it's part of a pre-written screenplay of life.

A screenplay is the script of a film, including acting instructions and scene directions. It's like a blueprint for how a movie will unfold.

To give a clearer perspective, think of people around you as actors in this movie with eventful turns, all written in the screenplay. While going through something similar myself, I realized we all are a part of this never-ending play, somewhere documented, engraved by what's above us all. Someone who knows everything the man is trying to seek.

Just like an actor, we have our script, a screenplay and a role, but what makes us different is how we set our equation with the characters around us, how we add our unique touch to everything we do, and how we play our role.

What's written is written, but we never lose the power on how we want to present our story, and our purpose in this performance.

When we understand that life is just a screenplay, we are able to detach our expectations from every character around us and acknowledge that they are meant to be where they are right now and do exactly what's written for them.

Accepting this fact is half the battle won, and the impact will improve your mental being.

You will become more mature in your understanding of being, and recognize that everyone is different and is meant to be the way they are. They certainly have no control over it, and neither do you.

When you are present on that stage in that moment, you begin to understand a blind man's point of view, who has never seen anything all his life—there is nothing inside which he can see, just black and grey shadows.

You discern what truly matters when you let yourself lose and live in the present.

Samantha may not like where she is right now, and maybe she wants to be set free, but the good news is that she's learned how to appreciate her life as it comes, like a screenplay.

When you find it hard to cope this time,

Recall that it's a vast screenplay, and we all are actors playing our parts.

FALSE MEMORY

Michael was sitting in a spaceship, looking down on Earth. At the time, he was at the peak in his industry—a tough, poised, strong, and brilliant man. Just 5 minutes of conversation with him, and anyone could deduce that he wasn't mainstream.

Sitting there, he was looking into the vast galaxy, glamorous stars, and mesmerizing beauty, almost captivating him into a trance; he was pondering about the events of his life that led him to this very moment. It wasn't just his dream anymore; it was his reality.

Somewhere, he put on his thinking cap, sitting 50 miles away from the earth's surface, hoping his entire life would gracefully place itself in front of his eyes like the magnificent consolations of stars he was surrounded with.

It's a scary, empty, and lifeless place to those who haven't dreamt of being here, but for him, it is exactly where he's always wanted to be.

He was looking through a circular window from his capsule, which gave a clear view of our planet Earth, and all he could think about was the first moment he knew he wanted to be an astronaut—the day he watched Sir Neil Armstrong's documentary for the first time.

I was sure that I wanted to be on that rocket, he thought to himself.

Hey there, it's Iris,

This story takes place in an impeccable setting, and it is about one of those men who's always known their purpose.

Perfect, isn't it?

Or is it?

Let me narrate to you a story set on a summer day in the 1980s when Michael was 5 years old.

It was a bright and pleasant Sunday; Michael and his family were in their backyard, enjoying their new tube pool.

After hours of playing in the pool and enjoying themselves with their dog Magnum, they decided to take a proper bath and gather in their family dining hall for lunch.

Michael had two siblings: his little sister, Maya, and a fraternal twin brother, Jim.

Michael felt tired and dehydrated after the exhausting gaming session in their backyard, so he was served lunch in his room, followed by a glass of glucose. Afterward, he took a long nap while his nana, parents, brother, and sister were having their Sunday steak-watching Neil Armstrong's documentary on BBC.

It was a happy, relaxed Sunday.

Did you notice something strange about that day?

The moment Micheal had remembered as the turning point when he decided to become an astronaut never actually happened.

So, what happened then?

Ten years later, he was lying on his nana's lap as she recalled that day.

"Do you remember the day we used our tube pool for the first time?" asked Nana, gently massaging her grandson's hair.

"Yes! What a lovely day that was!" replied Michael with a sense of nostalgia.

"You know, Michy, I always wanted to tell you that I believe you will be a successful astronaut one day, just like Neil Armstrong. I saw that zeal in your eyes that day, and I want you to know that I am always here for you whenever you need my support," assured Nana

Looking at her eyes with a baffled look, he was trying to rattle through his memory.

After a few seconds of pin-drop silence, Michael replied to her Nana, holding her hand with assurance,

"I will be, Nana. I love you."

"I love you, sweetheart," whispered Nana.

With the passing of time, Nana's memory aged rapidly, and she couldn't remember things precisely, so she recalled this little story about Michael's reaction to the documentary. Michael couldn't remember it at first, but then the memories came flooding as he heard Nana speak. He trusted her, and that trust unlocked the details of that day. He could remember the details of the event, and at that moment, he knew that he always wanted to be an astronaut.

There was no going back from that instant.

And he did become one. A successful one.

But why did it happen? And what will you ever receive by knowing about it, you might wonder.

It is the magic of false memory.

Technically, a false memory is a recollection that seems natural in your mind but is fabricated in part or whole. It is a mental experience mistakenly taken to be a veridical representation of an event from one's past.

Fuzzy-trace theory is a theory of cognition that explains the occurrence of false memories in our brains. It draws upon dual-trace conceptions to predict and explain cognitive phenomena, particularly memory and reasoning.

False memory occurs when we trust in something because we believe it happened, not that it happened or happened precisely that way. It is a scientific and psychological occurrence that leads us to believe in certain memories to such an extent that they actually start remembering them.

It's because the memories tend to distort and change over time; if you start believing something to be true, then your brain picks the bits and pieces of your incomplete puzzle to make sense of it as a whole. Usually, it happens because you either trust what you believe in or the person telling it to you.

Today, Michael is an astronaut because he accepted a false memory—one that gave him the direction he thought he always wanted to follow.

If you implant a false memory in your brain today, it will ultimately become your reality. I know it's hard to convince yourself to believe in something that seems unreal; however, Michael did not think he was passionate about being an astronaut until Nana made him believe he was.

It's not about what you aspire to achieve, but it's always about how strong your aspiration is.

Nothing is impossible; it's all about what you believe is true.

Little did he know, he was dreaming of horses and unicorns while the documentary played on their television. It takes time to accept and accomplish, but deep down, our faith in what we trust determines half of our success.

Try it yourself,

Believe you are, and you will become.

Sit down and cautiously make yourself believe in something your mind would otherwise reject by ascertaining that that's how it is meant to be; I promise you that years from that moment, you will have achieved it—and eventually forget that you ever had to make yourself believe in it. False memory might be a mistake or a syndrome, but it's all about perception and how you maximize it. No destination is too far once you know where you want to go.

Because you never know, even Neil Armstrong holds on to a false memory.

IT'S OKAY

Monica was shocked to see a little puppy roaming around in their kitchen. She shouted at the top of her lungs to call her twins. "Who brought it here? Don't you know how much I hate pets? Who will take care of him? How can you bring it here without asking?" She went on with her questions while Rick and Shina stood silently, looking down, hoping for a miracle that would allow them to keep the adorable golden retriever they had been looking after. To make matters worse, that little doggy peed on the kitchen floor when they were being scolded. *What a timing,* thought Rick to himself. "Ruffle! Stop… Don't! Don't!" exclaimed Shina in her sweet toddler voice, trying to sound strict.

"You named him?" interrogated their agitated mother.

"Isn't he so cute? He has been with us for 3 days now. He did not cause any trouble. I promise he won't do any harm. Please let us keep him. Look, he is so cute." Rick pleaded hastily.

"3 days!" replied Monica in shock, looking towards the puppy; all she could think of was to get him out of the house.

Shina was devastated when Monica put the puppy outside. She stopped eating and got very sick. She had been dreaming of keeping him for almost 3 months now. Ruffle used to see them in the park where they played with him. She thought of him like his little one. The kids were the happiest with him; his smile was like the sunshine, which lightened their day, and his adorable mannerisms kept them in awe. It was the happiest part of their day, as they received the affection that they'd been missing since Monica indulged herself in work to cope with the loss of her husband.

Monica was very concerned for her baby. She finally asked her why she had stopped eating, hoping to make her understand by initiating a conversation.

Shina replied, "Mamma, did you eat properly today?"

Monica shook her head in denial and said, "How can I, when you haven't?"

The little girl held her mother's hand and said, "Then how can I, till he doesn't?"

Ready for redemption, Monica decided to get the dog back. The children led her to the garden where they had met Ruffle every day. However, they were unsure if they'd find him since it had been three days since they'd last seen him. They waited, but as the minutes passed, they were met with nothing but disappointment.

They tried to find him everywhere near the park, but he was nowhere to be seen. As a few hours passed, Monica felt discomfort and concern for the first time, almost like what she had been feeling for Shina these past few days. They did not give up and kept on finding him. As the sun came down, so did the children's hopes, but Monica assured them they would find Ruffle. Almost home, Shina's irritation and anger increased, and she shouted at the top of her voice, "RUFFLE WHERE ARE YOU?!" Suddenly, small steps approached her from a box near the sewage outside their home. Monica's heart melted, and she broke into tears because

He never left.

John would see her baby for the first time in 3 years. He had been serving in the forces, far from home, during a difficult time for the country, where security was of great concern. His wife survived the pregnancy and raised their daughter alone for 3 years. It was a beautiful day today; she got ready, unlike any other day in years. Jasmine heard stories of her father every day before going to bed. She adored him and always wanted to meet him. Finally, the time arrived; Alisa was nervous, excited, and filled with so many emotions which have been building up for all these years; she just wanted to hug him and let him know that she waited for him every day since he left. Every second in the station felt like a lifetime until she saw her husband. Their eyes locked for a second, and he rushed into her arms, crying as all the pent-up emotions finally released. Just 2 minutes after his arrival, little hands tugged at the hem of his uniform to get noticed. All the tears, all his sorrow, everything fled like it wasn't the reality of his life for all these years after he saw the apple of his eye. He took her in his arms and looked at her like she was the most beautiful flower in a garden.

Her eyes were blue and big, just like her mother's, and her red cheeks were like her father's.

Weeks passed like a breeze of wind, and though the time felt like a day, the bond between Jasmine and John crossed all the years of parting, and it developed into something more meaningful than words can describe. On the final day before his departure, the happy family was visiting a mall; Jasmine wanted a red dress, which was too expensive for them. John was very sorry for the pay cut and promised Jasmine to buy her this dress when he returned. It was time to go again. Alisa couldn't stop her tears, but just like years before, she was ready to be strong again and wait till they saw him again. Jasmine held his finger entirely with her tiny hand and insisted, "Please, Daddy."

He planted a kiss on her forehead and moved towards the door abruptly. No bullets could have hurt him harder. A year later, he applied for a vacation, and it was approved. It was the happiest day, and this time, two sets of eyes waited to see his sight. Ten minutes before the train was scheduled to arrive, the speaker announced, ''Train 00654 has met with an accident. All the families are supposed to report to the office immediately." She ran to the office with her daughter, almost numb, like the world around her had stopped in a matter of seconds. There was the list of all the people who died on the spot, with John's name on the top—bringing their life to an endless pause.

Three months after his funeral, Alisa got the courage to open his bag.

And there was that same red dress she had wanted, with a note saying:

"Daddy always keeps his promise."

Mike and his older brother Lenard lived with their parents in the countryside, where they owned an apple farm. They grew lots of apples and earned their livelihood from them. Lenard had a habit of biting an apple before giving it to his baby brother.

Mike always made a face whenever that happens, feeling as though Lenard took the sweeter part for himself. As they grew older, Mike, an ambitious and intelligent kid, left for the city to make his name.

It took many struggles for him to create an identity from scratch in this new, fast-paced city, after finishing college. Meanwhile, Lenard took care of the family farm after their parents died. Both of them settled and used to meet once a year. Lenard's habit did not change, and it kept bothering Mike, but he never said anything to him as the younger one.

Years later, it was Mike and Nia's 25th marriage anniversary, and for the first time, Lenard visited the city with his daughters and wife to be present at his brother's marriage anniversary celebration. It was a great party; everybody thoroughly enjoyed the celebration. Lenard decided to stay a little longer. It had a purpose.

That Sunday morning, Mike was cleaning the shelf in the guest room when he accidentally saw an envelope with his initials. Lenard decided to give it to him while leaving for home.

Mike couldn't help but open it.

It read:

> *"Dear brother,*
>
> *When you were younger and wanted to go to the city for your education, you hardly had any money. Do you remember the college I always talked about? Well, I got in. I said I did not, but I did. The offer letter is still in my safe, untouched. But then it was either you or me. So, I stayed back. Today, all I ask from you is to help me so my daughters don't have to make that choice.*
>
> *Love,*
> *Len."*

Mike wiped his tears and left his room to see his brother in the dining hall offering him a bitten apple. "It's fresh and juicy; we got it from the farm," said Lenard.

He stopped him and took a bite from the side that his elder brother always kept for himself,

"It's tasteless!" Mike exclaimed.

"You always deserve the sweeter apple," said his brother.

Hey there, it's Iris,

These stories must have made you feel a little vulnerable, moved you in some way, or maybe there is a tear in your eye right now.

We are taught to be strong; sometimes, you keep it all in because you never want to appear weak. This is to assure you that your vulnerability is your strength to feel more than others could; it is your strength because you aren't afraid to face, accept, and express your emotions.

Most of all, all that you feel right now makes you more human than you were a few moments ago.

It reminds you that you are a beautiful combination of your emotions—good, flawed, positive, negative, complex, or straightforward. And *that's okay.*

PRESENT

Like every night, Mia was ready for her bedtime story, resting on her mother's lap and facing her so she could enjoy every expression her mother made while reciting the tale. But today was special: little Mia turned three, and it was her first year speaking. She had become more curious and eager to learn, her brain developing at an incredible pace; it was a beautiful and tender time in her life, and like any other parent, her mother wanted to make the most out of it. This time, Laila decided to recite a love story, wearing an extraordinary necklace her husband had gifted her.

Once upon a time, there lived a boy named Ted and a girl named Lisa. They met when they were very young, different but still alike; they were best friends, lovers, and everything for each other from the day they met. Eventually, they fell for each other deeply and got married. Lisa loved charm, sparkle, diamonds, and royalty, whereas Ted, let's say, was not into any of that; he lived and valued relations above all. They were like two pieces of a puzzle, different yet complete together. They lived in a hut with love, laughter, and comfort. Ted worked hard daily so Lisa got everything she had ever dreamed of and never had to compromise. Ever since she started dreaming, there was one thing on her wish list: a diamond necklace, a special one with platinum carving and polished stones. She always knew where to find it; she even tried saving for it, but life never allowed her to preserve it for long. Since they were young, Ted remembered how Lisa always talked about that necklace. She said that wearing it would make her the happiest alive. Like all her wishes, Ted heard this one, too. It was Lisa's 33rd birthday, Ted got her a present; it was the very necklace she had always wanted. Lisa was the happiest person on this planet, smiling and crying with joy; the sparkle of the necklace reflected in her eyes all that time. Ted admired her with a smile as if his whole world were before him. It was a *beautiful day indeed.*

Two weeks passed. On 21st June *2008, the sun shone brightly, yet there was darkness in the air because Ted never saw daylight again.*

Before passing, he left a note for Lisa, which said:

"Dear my love, I know we couldn't have borne the expenses, so I did not inform you about the infection that resulted from the kidney that I donated. My gut tells me I won't wake up to see your beautiful face again. I can feel it. I never thought it would grow this much. I love you and our baby to the moon and back. You know I can die for that smile. Yours, always and forever, Ted."

Just when the story concluded, Mia's little brain tried to process a perplexing thought in her naive, curious mind, and she asked in her innocent voice, "Is this a love story between Lisa and her love for the necklace, Mommy?"

There was silence between them, sharing all the secrets and all the lies, Lisa had deceived herself. After 3 years of running away from the guilt, finally, her love story came to an ending.

She looked towards the necklace today, and it was nothing... just chains.

REAL GOLD

You know the value of gold when you feel the metal; it's not as attractive as other minerals. Still, prices mean nothing when value is everything.

Hey there, it's Iris,

There lived two brothers who started identical business ventures together. The older brother sat on his seat and controlled the numbers, making sure that profits were on the rise; he was a highly ambitious and determined human being. The younger one prioritized human values above anything else and ensured that the employees felt that they had been taken care of. He hardly sat on his seat and made frequent visits to his employees on the shop floor; however, his profits weren't as high as his brother's, and sometimes he even sacrificed his earnings for the well-being of his employees. Five years later, the young brother's company is flourishing while the older one is figuring out a new start-up that survives the competition.

What do you think caused the older brother's downfall?

Mona and Nina were neighbours; Mona waited for Nina every day under a banyan tree, watching it grow every single day, while Nina finished her tuition classes; they used to meet to play at 5 p.m. One cold Autumn day, Nina was surprised to see that Mona wasn't waiting for her. She looked up towards Mona's house and saw her standing on the balcony, looking upset. Something must be wrong, she thought; this had never happened before. "What's wrong, Mona?" she asked.

"They cut the tree," Mona replied sorrowfully.

She is overreacting, Nina thought to herself, and left.

Why do you think there is such a stark difference in their thought process?

"You were very close to your grandfather. Remember when he fell so ill, and you stayed awake all night by his side, to be there for him in case he needed something? The kind of love you two shared, a bond unbreakable, always together no matter what," Duke's mother recalled at his grandfather's funeral.

Duke was informed about his grandfather's demise through a phone call and was asked to fly back to see his poppy for the last time. On his way back, all he could think about were the years of no calls to his grandfather. *I was too busy making my career; that's what Poppy would have wanted,* he assured himself. Everybody was deeply heartbroken and gave special attention to Duke because his sorrow was implied. He was indeed low-spirited, but the reason was not Grandad's passing but the realization that he couldn't feel that kind of remorse. What do you think made things different now?

IT'S EMPATHY.

Google gives a straightforward definition of empathy: "The ability to understand and share the feelings of another." However, there exists another perspective that we can view, an explanation with a solution of sorts.

Empathy is a feeling that arises when we end the physical distance we deliberately create between ourselves and others, whether it be things, people, or situations. It's really about feeling and seeing things closely in order to understand their growth and process to respect and appreciate it, which ultimately helps us give due consideration to its side of the story. It is like getting into a war knowing there can't be a winner or a loser in the beginning because you will ultimately see it for yourself.

Empathizing takes effort; however, it is paramount for personal growth and success. The young brother sacrificed short-term gains for long-lasting bonds; he cared to know them personally and valued their lives to understand their side of the story. In this way, the employees were no longer profit-making machines, but in fact, stories that mattered to him.

The little girl felt deeply connected with the tree and valued its growth and purpose, which made her understand its story; she understood the loss because she personally felt it.In the end, Duke kept his distance from his grandfather, because of which he never felt like he used to feel for him again.

Removing this distance is a sign of maturity because it's a long-term process that fosters patience and helps us attain extremely important but highly underrated qualities, which makes us more human than we are.

Just like gold, we value empathy only when we feel it ourselves. **Gold is an investment in a world full of diamonds. The question is, what do you choose?**

BIRYANI WITH LOVE

Preparing herself to sleep in pyjamas, Raina completed the task of writing her diary as instructed by her counselor. It always took a great deal of effort for her to write her emotions down on paper, but that was the whole point of therapy—to help make the young lady *feel* again. Six months ago, her father died in a car crash when she was writing her exam. She was thrilled during the exam as she knew the answers to every question. She was imagining having a celebration at home afterward, when she was called by the electronic speaker in the classroom. Completely perplexed, she was asked to sit by the headmaster before her heart was torn into several pieces.

Returning to an empty house, which was once a home, she fell into a motionless state. The girl's mother had run with her father because of religious differences and tied the knot. They had a beautiful marriage for 16 years until her mother died because of a heart attack. Aunt Rosy next door is the closest thing she had to a family. Her father planned everything for her dear daughter in case she was left alone, but the emotional burden took its toll on her, and her signs became evident.

Miss Rosy consulted her to a psychologist, and here we are back again to the present, looking at her diary with some doodles and a few words. That night was special though—not as ordinary as other days; it was a Wednesday, and just like every Wednesday, she wrote something.

This time, it was a page-long description of the special Wednesday Biryani topped with dry fruits. That was the key ingredient of the dish, something that distinguished her dad's handmade delicacy from anything else in the market, and most of all, it was made with love.

Just like all dads, her dad cared for her more than his own life, protected her, and especially after his wife's death, the two have been closer than ever. Each other was all they had, which was enough.

That hasn't been the case every Wednesday; she did improve over time—what started as a single line now filled an entire page.

At her monthly follow-up, the counselor asked Riana, "Why every Wednesday?" While narrating her story, Riana disclosed the special parcel that she had been receiving from someone with a note saying "To my daughter."

"Do you know where it is from?" asked Dr. Sharma.

"I never had the courage to find out," said Raina, her nervousness clear in her body language.

"Relax, my child; it's okay. You should find out," recommended the doctor.

For six months, she came back to a parcel with biryani topped with dry fruits just like her father used to make.

The parcel became her motivation to live, improving her state for many months. Although it tasted nothing like what her Abba made, that never stopped her from relishing every bite of that dish. It meant so much more to her. It meant the world to her to say the least.

After meeting the counsellor that day, Raina wasn't able to put her mind off the thought of knowing who had been sending her that parcel every Wednesday. Finally, she decided to contact her courier service and ask about the parcel's sender. They gave her an address.

Raina's diary (Sunday, 17th June 2008) – ***Reaching that address, I saw a man opening his shop early in the morning and bringing dry fruits from his shop. All I saw was that he opened the small packs and topped them on a tiffin full of biryani. Packed it nicely and handed it to the courier man with a note. I don't know, but I was too nervous to ask him why he was doing that. A week passed, and I received the biryani as usual. I found the courage to ask him about the parcel; I left for the shop and saw a new man sitting there. I asked for the man that I was looking for and briefed his appearance. Do you mean Aftab? Are you Adil's daughter? he enquired.***

I told him that I am her.

And the new shop owner just looked at me in some kind of relief. He asked me to sit in his office, and I did. The

man disclosed that my father used to buy dry fruits for biryani every Wednesday from their shop when he was an assistant manager here. He used to talk about how he wanted the freshest lot because it was for his daughter. He further added that he was extremely proud to know that I loved his Wednesday biryani.

Your father and Aftab were pretty close; they shared fewer words, but he always made sure that your dad received what he wanted.

After knowing about my father's demise, Aftab started making biryani for me and continued to send it to me so that I would never feel my father's absence. It made my heart melt, and my eyes were all wet with tears of realization of how he made efforts for me. He cared for me just like my dad would have. He was so thoughtful for doing that for me, to give me one light of hope, which has made me go on all this time. He doesn't even know what he has done for me. It's amazing how a stranger can come into your life and leave footprints inside your heart forever.

He is on his way to take his belongings; it's destiny that wants you two to meet, said the man. Just when he said this, Aftab arrived. I looked towards him and hugged him instantly. I felt Dad.

Features

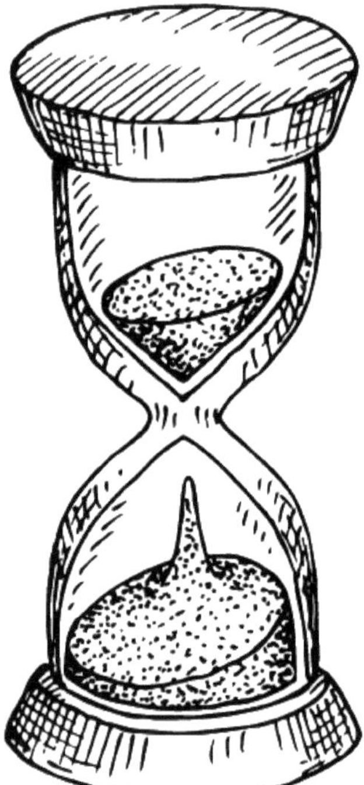

IT WAS NEVER ENOUGH

On a cold winter morning, seventy-year-old Maria lies in a bed in a hospital in New Brunswick, looking out the only window in the quiet room. It's almost Christmas, she thought, trying to remember the last time she was the happiest—fifty years ago. *What went wrong*, she thought to herself. Why doesn't she have everything she has ever wanted? Even after becoming the CEO of the multi-million-dollar company she once joined as an intern, why is she alone up there lying in the best room of the best hospital in the country, having the best services, feeling miserable because she was very, very lonely…

Hey there, it's Iris,

Have you ever felt that you would be happy once you reached a certain milestone, only to get there and realize you are not satisfied because you're already looking forward to your next goal?

Most of us have been there in life—or maybe still are—where nothing feels good enough. We work hard and keep working hard striving for something we desire, driven by a zeal that pushes us forward in life. Feeling this way is essential, but when it starts to affect your mental peace and becomes a toxic habit, that's when it is time to stop and reassess before it's too late.

Getting too worked up and thinking you will get everything in life someday is easy and a common problem as all of us have become a part of that rat race, but what you don't realize is all that you are missing by not enjoying the process of getting there. In most cases, it's the process in itself that teaches us most, and that's what makes it beautiful. It makes you grow, learn, evolve, and become something greater than you ever imagined you could be, and if you think about it, then that 'someone' is the very person you once wished to be.

Maria remembered the time when she was 20 years old, a young intern, full of life.

Today, she has one of the biggest regrets because, during this process, she forgot to live life for what truly matters.

After everything she had, she had the biggest regrets of feeling like nothing she did had ever been enough her entire life.

She enjoyed Christmas Eve with her family and friends—friends who faded away over the years, and family with whom she hardly spent time. She regrets not enjoying her life, something she holds on to in her final few hours.

She kept working too hard and got burned out, striving for something she couldn't quite understand. In doing so, she missed opportunities to enjoy what she had achieved.

I saw a video discussing what people regretted the most when taking their last breaths, and most revealed that they regretted working too hard.

They say that excess of anything is harmful, and that having a balance in life is all one must aspire for. I mean, nothing can be your *entire* life. It will always be a part of it.

Imagine your life like a salad; excess or less of something will affect that salad's whole texture, taste, and properties, making it something it is not supposed to be. A balance of proteins, carbs, fats, and everything else is essential to make your salad healthy. Likewise, having a bit of everything in your life is necessary to live it honestly.

I know that if you are a workaholic, then it can feel almost impossible to stop. It's like you feed on your work and have some fire burning inside you all the time. A fire to do something great in life is good only if you know when to stop and set your priorities right. But once you lose sight of where to stop, this can become an addiction. Eventually, you will look back and realize you are not enjoying life and all that it can offer.

I don't know if you get it today, but trust me, it will hit like a rock of regret one day because you will always want more and will never be satisfied with what you have in life. It's an endless cycle, you see.

Throughout my life, I've learned that what you once wanted may not be what you want today, and what you want today may not be something you'd like tomorrow.

Tomorrow and yesterday are not in our hands. What is in our hands is today, and it's a healthy habit to think of today because nothing is predictable. Even after you work so damn hard, what are the chances that you will achieve what you want? How do you know what you want is good for you?

That is when you will regret not living as much as you could have. This can be demotivating. However, that's a fact we should accept in order to live healthier and happier lives.

So, the next time you overthink about a tomorrow that might never come,

Leave your devices and sit on that chair in the garden to soak up the sun. And remind yourself that it was never enough.

STRENGTH

I saw this fantastic Netflix original, which was about a girl finding her way to fight back against the domestic violence and abuse that she was facing. When we see these things at a glance, it looks terrifying how someone can stay in this position and not protest. But the truth is, it is easier said than done.

Being in that position is traumatizing beyond words, and a person who has been in that girl's shoes could understand why she kept trying to fix her partner until she finally reached her breaking point.

Hey, there, it's Iris,

Watching that movie, I had tears in my eyes and goosebumps all over my body. I kept pondering, trying to make sense of that girl's behavior. Why did she not call out when her partner tried to hit her for the first time? I thought to myself.

The answer was straightforward: Strength.

Strength gives you courage, and courage gives you confidence—the confidence to say no and not put up with anything that doesn't resonate with your soul. I wonder, what is it about strength which is challenging to find? Let me break it down for you.

First, you have to start thinking about yourself, and you'll discover that you can do so much more, literally anything that you put your mind to. Then, all you need to do is break free of these self-created boundaries that never existed in the first place. Boundaries that kept you inside a box. The world is your oyster.

It's all in your mind, so it becomes almost impossible for a person in that position to stand up for themself. Breaking free from something you found endearing or comforting is scary, but sometimes it's necessary. When you finally decide, you should take time to understand the "Why." Why do you need to find courage in the first place? How do you think it can act as a guiding light moving forward?

I know this feeling is unsettling, and you must fight your heart when you do something for the first time. And keep fighting till you find the strength to resist anything that isn't good for you without a tear in your eye. You will start becoming more aware of yourself, everything around you, and most importantly, the reality. Finding that awareness will always give you the strength to fight everything for your happiness.

There are two sides to this coin; for some, struggling without courage can be depressing and unfortunate, but to me, it's the best gift God could ever give you—a chance to find strength after surviving everything without it, because now you know how you *don't* want your life to be.

The earlier you realize this, the better your life will become, and then it will only get better with time as the courage to fight for yourself will become a subconscious part of your being.

I remember achieving things I never thought I could or would have been able to do by finding strength. All you need to do is challenge yourself, like when you challenge yourself to be better every day or when you look at that steep mountain you must climb for the first time. Are you able to feel that feeling? The feeling you get in your stomach? It's such a big mountain; I have never done this before. What if I fall? What if I get tired in between and can't move further? What if the weather goes wrong, and it becomes almost impossible to move forward? What if I am out of supplies? What if I get an injury? So many *what-ifs* stop you from making that first step. Once you make that first step, you realize that you are natural at climbing mountains because you aced it the first time you tried. And then you know you don't want to stop because you have started feeling happy for the first time.

If you think about this, then honestly, there are so many things we shy away from and deny our joy because we don't have the willpower to fight our self-limiting thoughts.

Finding the strength to do many things is still a struggle for so many people. Since I have been on that boat, I can tell you that you should jump off that boat even if there is endless water around you. It's natural to think of death at that time, but you will swim through. I promise you will.

When you do, the waves will guide you to a magnificent island across the sea, which you could have never reached if you hadn't gone off that boat in the midst of the deep blue ocean. The still blue vastness that made you sit on that boat aimlessly.

I read this valuable write-up on the Speaking Tree, which made me wonder.

It said that once, a person decided to realize his dream. Only he didn't have enough strength to do it. Then he turned to his mother:

- Mother, help me!
- I would gladly help you, but I don't have it. And everything I have, I already give to you…

He asked a wise man:

- Master, tell me, where can I get the strength?
- It is said that it is on Everest. I couldn't find anything there except for the snowy winds. And when I came back, the time was irretrievably lost…

He asked the hermit:

- Holy Father, where to find the strength to realize my dream?
- In your prayers, my son. And if your dream is false, you will understand it and find peace in your prayers…

Who didn't the person ask? His search results only confused him even more.

- Why are you so confused? asked an older man passing by.
- Yes, I have a dream, good man. But I don't know where to find the strength to realize it. I asked everyone already, from Everest to hell. But no one could help me.
- Not everyone – a light flashed in an older man's eyes – did you ask yourself?

That girl in the movie never found the strength when other people kept telling her to stand up for herself, but only when something within her found it in herself.

It blows my mind to realize that the strength that helped me out was always inside me. I just needed to find it. No one can do that for you but yourself.

When you find courage, everything will change and look new. It will be overwhelming, and you will question your choices, at times the fear of the unfamiliar. But one day, very soon, you will look at yourself in the mirror and thank yourself, because you will see the person you have ever wished for, and yes, that person survived hell with strength.

THE QUOTE

I stumbled upon a quote that stayed with me, and I realized it's possibly one of the most profound quotes I have ever encountered. Let me share a thought with you.

"Sometimes, when you are in a dark place, you think you've been buried, but you've been planted."

The intensity of this line extends far beyond what's communicated; it's something most of us forget while progressing through the hurricanes of life.

We question where we are and believe we will be stuck in this position forever, which is never true.

Hey there, it's Iris,

I would like to give you a brief task.

Picture yourself stuck in a dark room with no space for light or any source of brightness.

Now imagine two scenarios: In the first, you stay still in that room and wait for someone to open the door; you convince yourself that staying put is safer, fearing that any movement might lead you to step on something sharp or fall. It feels more comforting to wait than to make any move.

In the second scenario, you are in the same dark room. You don't stand still but rather analyze the situation and move because the chances that someone might come and open the door are always 50/50. As expected, you get hurt by a nail while touching the walls to find a way. But then, you realize that the pin is on a wooden piece that closes the only window in the room.

So now you know that you don't have to wait for someone to come, and there is a way out.

This situation is symbolic of how sometimes we are trapped in situations where a solution seems impossible. We get paralyzed with fear, thinking we might end up in a worse position than before. Take the risk anyway.

Likewise, we may never know that what appears to be a dark, hopeless place with no escape in the depths of the land is where we are planted to bloom when we make efforts and develop the willingness to grow. In this process, the environment is everything.

A seed will never sprout unless it's given sufficient light, water, and manure to thrive. So, it is advised to be aware of everything you subject yourself to while you seek a way out of that dark room. Are the negative thoughts and constant voices in your head telling you that there is no escape?

We hear great stories of people who fought battles and achieved extraordinary heights. These fascinating stories aren't just tales, they are experiences for us to learn from and find meaning in. One such story is that of Sir Benjamin Franklin.

We all know him as an American polymath who was active as a writer, scientist, inventor, statesman, diplomat, printer, publisher, and political philosopher. But what many don't know is that when he was just ten years old, his family could no longer afford to send him to school, and things were so worse that they even had to live in a van to survive; he was in a dark place. He could get into any unconstructive or wrong path and make a living, but he understood that this breaking point was his gateway to something bigger—and he took action. He didn't wait for someone to hold his hand but moved forward on his own.

Financial concerns didn't stop him from pursuing his education because he read a lot and taught himself. He educated himself because of his hunger for education. Today, the world knows him as the man who invented the lightning rod and bifocals, and as the founding father of the United States.

His case was no exception; thousands face similar situations every day. What makes him unique is that he never found himself helpless in that state and accepted it as his permanent reality.

Resilience is the cornerstone of growth and innovation. If Sir Benjamin Franklin had viewed the world in a different way, American history would be very different from what it is today, and the world wouldn't have been blessed with his glorious inventions.

I'm not saying that picking yourself up from that place is easy. It takes guts, determination, and a vision of where you want to see yourself and what you want. Take your time, pick yourself up, and do something about it. You'll be surprised to receive more than you ever expected.

So always remember that when you are in a dark place in your life,

Take action, and leave the rest to the magic of time.

THE PACE

A few days ago, I saw a little pup walking on a rocky street. The little creature was too small for the stone in his path, and he kept stumbling with every step. It was beyond his comprehension; maybe the poor thing even thought the rocks were placed there deliberately to hinder him. At times, he would pause on the road in deep thought, but that didn't stop him from standing up again, wagging his tail, and moving forward to the beat of his own melody.

He fell repeatedly, yet every time, he started walking again till he eventually started enjoying the journey; that's when he began to avoid the rocks. He understood which way he was meant to go so he could avoid the rocks, and that's precisely when he started running at a fast pace. Then he reached his parents, who were expecting him on that street.

Ultimately, I saw him playing with his brother and sisters so happily, and that beautiful sight will remain captured in my consciousness forever.

Hey there, it's Iris,

Time tells and heals; time gives you lessons you would never learn otherwise.

We have heard this saying many times before, and know it to be true, yet sometimes, it's hard to understand this extremely simple logic.

We underestimate the power of time, what happens in our lives, and why exactly it happens the way it does because we are too impatient to understand the power of what's above us all.

Trust me, it's not only you, all of us have been there at some point in our lives, and it all happens for a reason, at its own unique pace.

I have witnessed many things happening with me, and to the people around me, and I never understood why the world is the way it is, why people are the way they are, or what I can ever learn from these experiences, which have affected me so deeply.

When going up the steep hill, one must know that one single misstep can cause you to fall.

There is another thing we often forget: that each misstep teaches us exactly where not to stand, which increases our chances of standing on the highest peak a little longer, or maybe even discovering the right way to stand over there firmly until the sun finally kisses the dusk, leaving us to enjoy the sunset with peace, contentment, and love in our hearts.

People and experiences are complex, and sometimes, we feel they are the way we thought them to be; we assume they feel the same way we do, simply because we have real intentions behind our actions. Walking that path with that little puppy, I have learned lessons the hard way myself.

It's not easy to come to these realizations; maybe age doesn't define when you genuinely understand them. Still, the natural way to learn these lessons is by being true to ourselves, because only then can we view things, perspectives, people, and experiences through an unfiltered lens of our own.

When that happens, everything starts to come together. Then, two and two combine and make sense; all the pieces come together and make us realize why it was meant to be that way. Maktub, like Paola, has put it beautifully is the faith, that it is all written and everything that happens to you is a part of your destiny.

There was a time when I used to question myself, who I am, and why things are the way they are, but like that little pup, I kept falling but got back up again and learned a lesson every single time, from people, from experiences, and most importantly from myself.

It's never easy to be true to your character in a circus like this, where people play characters they have been made to play, but it's essential for realization, and realization is not everyone's cup of tea.

As I started linking events in life, I came to a point where it all made sense; all that happened to me made sense, and it still does. I look forward to falling and standing back up, knowing it was meant to be this way.

It's not just an ordinary person like me, but even the greatest of legends who advocate for the pace of failures and cherish them as a learning experience; Micheal Jordan, when he talks about failures, puts it very rightly, "*I have missed more than 9,000 shots in my career. I have lost almost 300 games. On 26 occasions, I have been entrusted to take the winning shot, and I missed it. I have failed over and over and over in life, and that's why I succeed.*"

Our universe works in unique ways; it makes us fall when we are meant to fall and teaches us what we are meant to know at each point in our lives.

So, the next time you wonder,

Is this just how life is, or is it a phase?

Move forward and enjoy the pace.

YOUS

Unaware of the surprise, a hundred people were asked to enter a room.

Once, a group of a hundred people attended a seminar, and the speaker addressing the audience decided to do a group activity involving balloons. Each person was handed a balloon and was asked to write their name on it using a marker. All the balloons were randomly placed in another room, and everyone was asked to find the balloon with their name on it within five minutes. Everyone was searching for their names frantically, colliding with each other, causing utter chaos. For obvious reasons, no one was able to find their balloons. Now, the speaker asked the crowd to randomly collect a balloon and give it to the person whose name was written on it, and within minutes, everyone had their balloon.

Hey there, it's Iris,

When we are unhappy, we struggle to find inspiration in anything we love and face toxic emotions every day. They are all a part of the self-created thoughts in our brains. When we tell ourselves something is true, it eventually becomes true for us sooner or later. So, I am not implying that your problems are unreal, but they are the birth of your impressions.

It took a life-changing event for me to come to a point where I can truly say that I am happy today and intend to make the most of what I have with gratitude.

I know where I was, and I strongly believe that any of you can be in that position right now, so through this, I intend to put a smile on your face and hope that it all has a purpose.

Do you know what the speaker said at the end of the activity?

He said, "Exactly, this is happening in our lives. Everyone is frantically looking for happiness, not knowing where it is. Our happiness lies in other people's happiness—give them happiness, and you will get happiness."

Yes, he is right, and this is precisely what I learned towards the end of this phase in my life, but there is a twist, something we fail to understand so much that we end up in this ever-growing vicious cycle of expectations and worries.

Do you remember the time when you were a child? So happy and gay, smiling at strangers and finding laughter in even the slightest of things. Do you ever wonder where that person is?

That child is inside you and will always be. All he needs is a sign to know you are again free of worries and expectations!

Somewhere, it all starts with YOUS. This is a made-up word to put 'YOU' and 'US' together, emphasizing the importance of 'YOU' first embracing the 'US.'

No matter how hard you try to be someone else, living another life for people you want to be liked by, there will always be a point where you will feel unloved and unhappy, and this is no one's fault but yours because, in the course of life, we tend to not truly love ourselves, accept ourselves entirely, and be the master of our own life.

People and energies will always try hard to conquer your inner peace; ignore them, because they aren't worth it anyway. Once you are satisfied and at peace, you attract positivity and the right energy from those around you. You receive and give love to the ones close to you without pushing yourself. In other words, you become like a flowing river dancing down the hill and gently kissing every rock that welcomes it.

At the end of the day, it all starts in your head, and if you tell yourself that you won't let anyone take your love and positivity away from you, then even if the sharp and rugged rocks come by, you will still kiss them gently, and they'll let you go with more vigor and lessons.

Love and compassion are strong emotions; they are felt and appreciated by the right ones around you; hence, you receive and give the love you think you deserve.

Life becomes beautiful; trust me, there is no gift more significant than a life full of peace and contentment.

Yes, inner harmony and joy are of supreme importance, but at the same time, it is essential to understand that love is a two-way street.

So just like the subtle difference between what the speaker said and how it's achieved, there is indeed another catch to loving yourself and being happy in yourself—that is, you must appreciate your own energy and accept your flaws, work on them, and know that love and commitment involve sacrifices as well.

This makes you a beautiful human, not a selfish monster since it is easy to cross this line without realizing its consequences.

So, whenever you feel there is too much negativity out there, Look inside and radiate your cheer.

It's contagious.

THAT CHAIR

I felt sad that I was alone on the balcony of my new house in a new city, unaware of what lay ahead.

Slowly, I sipped a cup of coffee I had made for myself, and tried to make sense of the emotions swirling inside me. I found myself questioning and answering everything I have ever done, like I had all the time in the world. As the storming rain rushed down the dark clouds, so did my tears.

Hey, there, it's Iris,

Today, I want to share a glimpse of my thoughts while I ponder looking at that rain,

And trust me, regardless of where you are, it will help you—if not today, then tomorrow.

I have so much to say yet at the same time, nothing to say at all. I want so much to happen without wanting to see it.

I want to sit on that chair and watch the dark clouds as they cry beautiful droplets of relief.

I want to take a deep breath, knowing everything will make sense one day.

I have been feeling so many emotions that I've never felt before while moving to a new city, leaving my home for the first time, being surrounded by new people and a new environment. Everyday, I'm learning so much, not just about the world around me, but also about myself that it is almost impossible to comprehend what it all means.

Sometimes, I feel like I'm missing home, homesickness as they call it, and my days become gloomy like rainy days; other days, I feel free, like I'm the master of my own life—a liberating feeling as they call it, and my days develop into a picnic in a pleasant day. Regardless, between all these conflicting feelings every day, I've genuinely realized that feelings are life's biggest paradox.

A paradox is different from our opinion; it's like we have all the reasons to believe what we think is true, but still, it is not valid, and the reason for why it is false stands beyond the understanding of the tiny human brain.

Feelings that overwhelm us are just like paradoxes, providing grounds and rationale to every possible reason why feeling what you feel is true, even though what you felt just moments ago may contradict what we think now.

Sitting far away from family, I suddenly recall what made home feel like *home*—the value of every sour and sweet memory. At the same time, I understand that I can figure out life now, do what I want, and finally experience what it is like to be independent.

But then, life is a never-ending motion, and motion suggests that an object is at different places at different times, and when you are at various locations at various times, then nothing is inherently right or wrong; what matters is where you are at the time.

Sometimes, I wonder how I will ever adjust to this new setting, how I will be at peace with shifts, knowing that life is all about change. Just then, I sensed a cool breeze of wind, assuring me that I was adjusting to this new setting and finding solace. Eventually, I felt at ease, like a burden of bitterness had lifted from my shoulders; I was breathing a bit more freely now as the cool droplets gently touched my cheeks.

I was present here, present in my reality.

I have come to accept that this is life's biggest lesson, because being present is the single most important feeling. It is as simple as it sounds, without paradoxes or complications.

I strongly believe in the power of positive affirmations and how they tend to greatly influence how we perceive life and emotions, so now I allow myself to feel my feelings no matter what they are and let the universe speak to me in that moment.

Looking at the raindrops, I now see nothing but delightful dancing-drops eagerly waiting to kiss the ground.

In that instance, I appreciated the simple joy of sitting on that chair, sipping my cup of coffee on my balcony in this new city, and enjoying my company.

DIS-ASSOCIATE

In this age of the internet, information is readily available on any topic; the real question is what you choose to learn.

Like most individuals, I have been hooked on YouTube for a long time, trying to explore new ideas and see what's happening around the world with just a click. A YouTube channel caught my eye, which aimed to educate everyone about a condition called Dissociative Identity Disorder (DID). The way she educated and shared her life experiences with this disorder captivated me and I found myself watching all that she had to offer. For those of you who aren't aware of DID, scientifically, it is a disorder characterized by the presence of two or more distinct personality states. Dissociative Identity Disorder is usually a reaction to trauma as a way to help a person avoid bad memories. It is characterized by the presence of two or more distinct personality identities. Each may have a unique name, personal history, and characteristics.

Hey there, it's Iris,

Humans possess scientifically proven capabilities to cope with life's challenges, even when it feels unbearable.

Without delving too deeply into the concepts and technical aspects of DID, it can simply be understood as a coping mechanism of your brain that separates you from a painful memory or trauma so you can forget them and continue to exist, survive, and move on.

Eventually, your mind starts working in a way where, unlike an average individual with cohesive memory, individuals with multiple personalities have numerous unique identities and memories of every personality that develop over a lifetime. So, the personalities do not remember each other's memories at all, and that's what DID is all about in the most uncomplicated way.

So, what is there to learn from a rare disorder like this? Here, I would like to emphasize a statement mentioned earlier: "It's all about what we choose to learn."

What we can learn is how people deal with breaking points in their lives, and a disorder like this is just a reminder that there is nothing in life that cannot be dealt with pride and composure, knowing one can indeed move on and survive it through.

Think about it, if you are reading this today, you have already survived one of the greatest calamities of all time: the virus. You should be proud of yourself and know that you are strong enough to face whatever life has to deliver at any point.

This disorder is indeed rare. However, it occurs in humans, reminding us that we can separate ourselves from any distressing experience.

It helps us understand that life goes on like a flowing river regardless of the complex and heavy pebbles that come its way.

For a moment, imagine a river and how its current and rigor increases with every rock clash. Isn't that beautiful?

We all have this power inside, but sometimes the memories remind us of the experiences repeatedly, which is why our case is different from someone with DID. They don't remember, but we do.

We can't stop the memories, but we can learn how to manage them through a simple exercise: talking.

Something as simple as talking is a form of therapy, a solution for them and us.

Talking provides a perspective on how to look at situations, as we often tend to realize things while we speak. It allows a person to detach from or learn from a memory, helping them move on.

For the critics and suspects of DID, even Freud's ideas advocate this phenomenon. I don't deny that he has been criticized for some of his work, and many of his contributions are outdated and irrational, but that doesn't change the fact that some of his theories have been thought-provoking and valuable, just like his theory on unconscious mind and dynamics, and multiple personalities systems which subtly offer an explanation for dissociative identity disorder.

There was a man who lost his house and family to a fire at home while he was sitting at his office desk, unaware that his life was going to change.

Devastated and shattered into pieces, he broke and burst into tears knowing what had happened, and the burden of not being able to protect his family was immense. He knew that he would not be able to survive through this burden and decided to end his life. But just as he was about to take that step, he noticed a half-torn piece of paper with a drawing that his child had made for a school competition captioned: "My daddy is my hero. He is strong and he is powerful."

He stopped, as he realized that he was strong, just as his little princess had always believed.

Yes, it took a lot of effort and quite a few therapy sessions to accept the truth and gain a different perspective on what happened. He finally accepted that he had nothing to do with the fire, and there was no way he could have stopped it from happening.

Ten years later, he advocates for mental health and mindfulness and delivers TED talks to raise awareness about how it's possible to move on from events you think will forever haunt your existence. This Jacob has a different identity from the Jacob 10 years ago because he grew and learned to cope with the loss with elegance.

You know, becoming like Jacob can feel like a tough road, but there is one thing you must know—while living with that burden feels like fate, remind yourself that you can always be free.

All it takes is to disassociate.

You never have to live with it.

A LESSON

Hey there, it's Iris,

Once upon a time, there lived two brothers, Iqbal and Ibraham, who dwelled in the slums on the outskirts of the capital city. They were rag pickers, but they preferred being addressed as "waste managers."

A waste manager toured the site once a month, and they heard everyone call him that. *We are also doing the same work,* thought Ibraham. Since then, they have been the new waste managers of their slum, taking great pride in it.

Speaking of being proud, their home was like a shed made of huge plastic paper and many sticks leveled to give the space a structure. It was less than the maximum number of households in Shabad. With a family of five, they managed to scrape together enough for a daily meal. They struggled, yet somehow, they were still so happy.

If we go by Google, happiness is defined as the feeling of pleasure or contentment. If happiness is that simple, why do we struggle to find it?

That's because we raised this question in the first place.

It's not complicated, but we make it to be.

There are numerous theories on happiness, from the concept of ikigai to Neil Pasricha's equation for happiness. Everyone is trying to discover happiness when, in reality, it has constantly been there within us.

The real challenge is recognizing that happiness is already there, waiting to illuminate our spirit.

For a brief amount of time, I wasn't fulfilled in my writing; it felt empty, and something was lacking in my content.

The answer was *hope.*

It needed possibility.

And hope is the sole most powerful force that unifies this world concurrently into one happy place.

To those of you who think that Iqbal and Ibraham were happy with what they had, you are wrong. They were cheerful because they had hope—hope that they would prosper into something better than what they were; they hoped for a meal every day, they were satisfied that they had a roof over their heads to fight seasons, and most significantly of all, they were happy to live another day driven by hope.

That's what kept them optimistic, Hope.

Maybe I wasn't feeling it, but I battled to find inspiration and hope.

Just like all of us do at some point in life. We spend hours searching for that one moment to hold on to, the one we can call hopeful.

Finally, I realized that the moment I opened my eyes that day, I was grateful for this life, and during breakfast, I was satisfied that I was able to fulfill my hunger; looking at my parents and my dog that evening. I felt a sense of relief and comfort from their valuable presence around me, and unknowingly there came to pass so many events throughout the day, which extended hope in some shape or form while I foolishly kept looking for that defining moment every minute.

No minute defines hope; it is there, and it grows.

It unfolds with you, for you, and around you. You get so used to it that you stop noticing.

At that moment, I realized that I had been feeling hopeful every single day, and this is the inspiration for what I write today. I feel happy sharing this experience with you because it is hopeful and ascertains the very foundation of our existence.

We need to know that hope lives inside and around us all.

We struggle to find it, just like I did. Just like anybody else would. There are gloomy times in life when it feels like a dead end.

Nevertheless, we must know that,
Hope is happiness

Happiness is Hope.

And when you are busy finding it everywhere

Remember,

It's right there inside you, in here.

I-M-MORTAL

She was always remembered at every family gathering when her daughter arrived. Her every action, all her mannerisms, and the conversations that she had reminded me of her mother. Like her mother, she was the heart of all gatherings, and no one in the room could help but enjoy her presence. Even after 10 years since Aunt Mary's demise, she lived on in her daughter and in every person she met throughout her lifetime.

Hey there, it's Iris,

Since childhood, we have been aware of our mortality, yet we cling to theories that promise immortality. I know it can surprise many of you, and I don't deny that it's utterly subjective depending on how you perceive it. Still, if you welcome this conjecture with an open heart and mind, then I am sure you will appreciate a more significant responsibility, which is much more than life itself. For this, it's vital to understand who you are.

Throughout our lives, we all go through remarkable physical changes from a baby to an adult, and ultimately, we grow grey hair with a 180-centimeter-high structure.

Biologically, our cells get replaced every 20 years, meaning there is no sign of memory between these age brackets, due to which when you look back, you won't be able to recall who you were 20 years ago. Generally, compliments made on physical characteristics feel rather superficial or emotionally detached because somewhere deep down, we know that we are much more than what others can see.

Who am I?

Now imagine you lost your memory; you don't remember a single experience of your life… will you still be you? The answer is yes. It is still you.

If you had two options today: keeping your memory intact while being an entirely differently responsive individual, or losing your entire memory but still holding the same values as before, most of us will choose the latter.

Why do you think that is? Because in the fullness of time, although our names stay the same, it is our character—our values, beliefs, and principles—that truly define who we are.

Losing your body and mind into ashes doesn't cease your existence because your character makes your identity; it stays and lives on forever. Delighted with joy, Rosy did not realize that just like her, her mother was also reminded of her mother.

There lived two brothers—identical twins. They went to the same school and almost had the same experiences. On the surface, no one could ever identify any difference between them. However, after just a few minutes of conversation, people found themselves naturally drawn more to Peter.

They were the same, yet so different. Peter was a man of character and values, while Henry contrasted his brother's personality. Years have passed since they left, yet everyone in their family remembers Peter; many have inherited so many of his traits without realizing. After all these years, while Uncle Henry is just in the frames and photographs, Peter lives in the family hall forever.

We all remember Princess Diana for her beauty, but somewhere, we are subconsciously inclined towards the purity of her character—her values, and the innocence she radiated. Regardless of her mesmerizing beauty, her aura stays in the hearts of billions forever.

Only do what your heart tells you – Princess Diana

It's natural to wonder what you will gain from learning about this truth while you live, and I have two answers that hold equal importance. First, when you know you are much more than how you look and what you see, it doesn't confine you to these shallow labels because it's not who you are, nor can it ever be, and the second reason is much of a reminder to focus on what matters.

Enhancing your character is an underrated and unsaid duty that begins the moment we take our first breath. Somehow, our urge to be immortal will remind us of our mortality; it's contradicting, but once understood deeply, it will ensure that you are remembered for the good you did in the limited time of your continuance.

So now, when you wish to live on forever… remind yourself that your time on this planet is limited; what matters is how you live while you have a chance to mark your footprint.

QUEST

In our beloved fairy tale *Alice in Wonderland*, Alice comes to a fork in the road, unsure of where to go. When the cat asks her where she wants to go, Alice replies, "I don't know about this place." The cat responds with a smile, "If you don't know where you want to go, any road will take you there.'

Hey there, it's Iris,

As a writer, it is easy to be short of ideas; when I do have them, it becomes difficult to turn them into pieces of writing I am truly convinced of. It starts bothering me to the extent that I have dreams about them. During times where I've experienced a creativity drought, I questioned whether life had probably pushed me away from my craft, and I started doubting what I was doing. Once, when I was feeling this way, I was determined to find a solution and know what was happening to me. That morning, I learned about writer's block—a mental block that prevents you from embracing your creativity as you chase an unattainable ideal of perfection; failures never solve their true purpose in the process and only make the person overly cautious.

Introspecting the truth about what was stopping me was a point of self-analysis since I have never been a person who believes in the illusion of perfection.

Pondering, I realized the countless times we forgo something in life looking for perfection and never actually enjoy the process of receiving the greatest gift of failure.

Every time you fail, you not only learn what doesn't work, but also realize that it was through those failures that you were finally led to where you're meant to be.

I read a short story about a lady who starved for body perfection. She always had that ideal body in mind that she was never able to achieve. One day, her dear friend, who back in town after 8 years, invited her to a party where they could spend some time together; she was skeptical about whether to go or not because she was self-conscious about her body and didn't want to wear baggy clothes in front of other people to hide her flaws. Regretfully, she said, "I stayed home running as hard as I could on the treadmill in my parent's basement, trying to burn calories as if I'll lose all my fat in one day; it was my birthday that day," she added.

Perfection is an unattainable goal that continues to make so many people insecure every day, preventing us from creating something of our own, even if just for a moment. In that interview, she admitted that she wished she had never strived for perfection, and regretted missing out on living the moments and experiences she could have forever cherished.

We attempt to endeavor perfectionism in fear of being judged. Calling the struggle to perfection an act of 'improvement' is like comparing the moon to the sun. It looks the same from the outside but is entirely different from the inside; you can never attain the sun. You might burn miles away from it, just as Sir Neil Armstrong gracefully proves the latter.

Gazing deep into that unachievable goal, we forget to fail, learn, stand up, fail, learn, stand up.... Until we get something we call of our own, we can connect the dots, thank every failure, and bid goodbye with a promise to see each other again.

The fear of failure blinds us from acknowledging how beautifully our journey is unfolding before our eyes. We all have been and will continue to be there as long as we live.

Thomas Edison failed a thousand times before inventing the bulb. When asked what he feels about failing so many times, he said, "I feel lucky to have failed a thousand times because each time I discovered one new way that a bulb can't be made." Until today, we see improved versions of the bulb, which implies that even his invention wasn't perfect. It exists as something he could call his own, and though we now have countless better versions of this light source, the iconic bulb remains the fundamental of all inventions. Think about what would have happened if Sir Thomas Edison had kept struggling for perfection; a never-ending quest would have stopped him from blessing us with his contribution.

Similarly, if Alice keeps on searching for a perfect path, she will never be able to take the wrong turns and know exactly where *not* to go to reach where she is meant to be.

It's not hard to stop running behind perfection; all it takes is to stand where you are and trust that whatever follows will take you exactly where you should be, just like this chapter's inspiration was in my struggle to find the idea itself.

So, the next time you see a dead-end at the end of a fork, tell yourself it's nothing, just another writer's block.

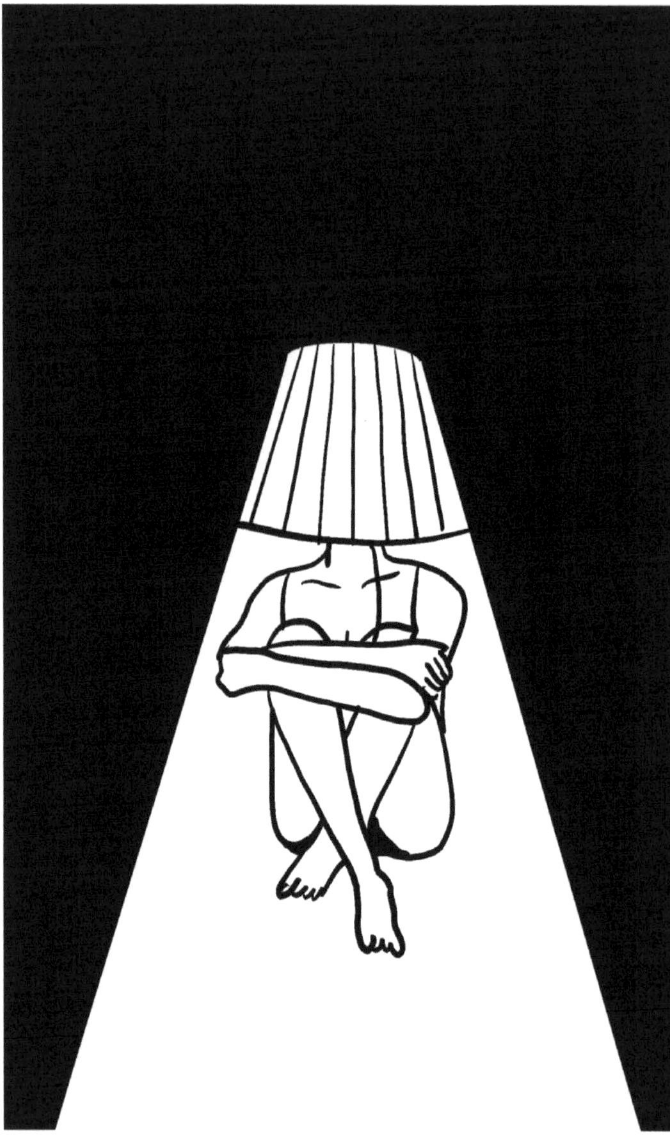

SHUSH

After a massive quarrel with her parents, Sara stormed out of her house to take a brisk walk, hoping to release some tension, and get some fresh air. As she walked down the familiar streets, the sounds of birds chirping, voices in the distance, and the occasional vehicles passing by filled the air. She happened to take a wrong turn, and the pace of her steps slowed. Just five minutes into her walk, she started feeling regret for talking the way she did; suddenly, her parent's perspective came into the picture and made more sense to her than it ever did. *That's a first,* she thought to herself. Standing with discomfort on that motionless path where she couldn't hear anyone except herself.

Hey there, it's Iris,

I have a question for you; it doesn't have a perfect answer, just an explanation that can be subjective, but it is necessary to have your version of the answer.

So, what is Silence?

For me, Silence is in those few moments we experience when we wake up, the first feeling of stillness in the morning before we dive into our never-ending to-do list for the day. It is inside us all, and that silence is very personal—an inner calling, almost like an opportunity to introspect. Not only that; it's the basis of solving the puzzle of life, connecting the dots, and making sense of your entirety. They are precious moments with self.

I tried embracing silence and felt curious about the most silent place on earth. Browsing through, I had visions of forests, mountain peaks, between the seas, etc., in my head, but to my surprise, it wasn't what I thought it would be; instead, it was a room at Microsoft's headquarters in Washington. The unique technology makes the room so quiet that a person can hear his heartbeat and even the cracking of bones while making a move after a point of time. Fascinated by the silence between the chaos, I continued reading the article and delved deeper into it.

A thought-provoking fact caught my eye, mentioning a group of people who were interviewed after visiting the room. Few of them found it calming and even cried in peace, while others felt nauseous and started throwing up. The stark difference in reactions captivated me, and I couldn't help but reflect on why that was.

Well, that's my version; most of us are running a race, trying to be as productive as possible. Failing to recognize something as basic as our presence and appreciating the fact that we are one of the most intelligent beings on earth or we were able to swim through a million sperms to be the lucky ones to things which are subject to self-awareness like knowing what you always do but are too ignorant to appreciate. We try to comfort ourselves between the noises to move away from our inner selves, deliberately never wanting to face what's happening inside us, with us, or within us.

It's in you.

Hearing every breath, heartbeat, and movement of your bones reminds people of their presence, like peeping into a room you have been asked to stay away from—an unpleasant reality check that pulls you away from the world into somewhere deep inside. Sara knew that silence challenged her to introspect and connect the dots to make sense of her parents' arguments. Your spirit knows the answer to all your questions, even to things you have never thought of before; it's inside you calling out your name, but to hear the calling, you need to stop the noise and Shush.

To some of you, spending some time with your silence might not sound like the best idea… I mean, who has time for that? Instead, talk your problems out or seek advice from someone you trust.

The good news is, you don't need a counselor because you have the power to find a solution within yourself. Believe it or not, Silence isn't empty. It is full of answers. The quieter it is, the more you can hear things you haven't been able to listen to.

Be it German scripts saying, "Sprechen est Silber, Schweigen ist golden"— meaning "Speech is silver, Silence is golden"—or the Indian Scriptures saying "Yogasya Pratamam dwaram vaang nirodha," meaning, "You won't find the pearl you're looking for if you constantly keep churning the ocean water." You need to let stillness set in for the pearl to appear. If you read any scripture, all of them mention the importance of silence and how it contributes to realizing things we tend to ignore in the commotion of life. As we mature and age, we come to understand the extent of its importance, and how so many things would have been positively different if we had heard ourselves in silence.

Now, whenever you end up walking too fast, take a 'wrong turn' and get comfortable with your silence.

CREATOR

There are endless theories revolving around a particular concept; some may deny it, while some may agree; the probability of its occurrence is a definite one. Perfect chances always remain because we make theories based on our assumptions, and in the fullness of time, the reality lies in one of them.

Hey there, it's Iris,

The mystery of sleep, dreams, illusions, and reality is just as entrancing as any other concept that revolves around the unknown. Psychology, medicine, and science have dedicated their lives to solving this tedious puzzle. As time passes, another fascinating theory appears to solve the mystery of sleep and dreams.

I have always been intrigued by the enigma of dreams—what dreams are, and where we go when we sleep. I was mildly convinced by a particular theory, that cannot harm and only do good. The theory suggests that our reality, as we call it, is a dream that we experience throughout our lives, and when we die, we are transported back to THE REALITY, which some may know as the "Afterlife."

Why would I call my reality a dream?

It's because we build our dreams with the magic of our subconscious and conscious minds. Dreams are the total combination of what we surround ourselves with, be it thoughts, people, energy, or anything else. Believing that our reality is a dream, a fantasy we are in, makes us the creator of however we want to perceive it.

I stumbled upon an inspiring story in Reader's Digest about a lady from Asia who was a teacher and lived in a dead marriage for nine long years. After leaving her husband, she discovered that he had been cheating on her for months. She desperately wanted to create her identity and start over, so she took a giant leap and went to New York City with two duffel bags and not a single friend or family member in sight. Moving to the States, she started working in social media for big brands like Yahoo!, Duane Reade, and Moët. She later remarried a fantastic man. "You are in control of your fate," she says! I call it driving your dream.

Just think about the limitless possibilities we can generate by surrounding ourselves with the right system to obtain it. That means you are an architect of your life with a blueprint you choose.

Remember how we all "dream" about something as stupid as being a superhero? Well, the good news is you can be one in reality. If you believe and put in the sufficient effort, then you *are* a superhero because, in the end, it's all a dream.

The dream of life is an illusion, and everyone lives the reality he or she creates. In times when the summit is too high, tell yourself it's a dream, and you can fly.

SHADOW'S PLAY

I was frantically looking for my anti-glare glasses, running late for an online meeting scheduled. I tried finding it everywhere, but then the power went out, and my restlessness reached its peak. Just then, my father walked by holding a torch in his hands. As the light from the torch cast my shadow, I saw it—there they were—my glasses! There was an indistinct shape of something resembling specs on my head. I was trying to find it all this time while they had simply been on my head all along. "Good, the torch helped," said my dad.

Hey there, it's Iris,

We often try to find what's wrong with us and what it is we can't see that holds us back from becoming a better version of ourselves. At some point, we all wish to be better and finer in our lives because regardless of how cruel this world gets, we all possess a subtle sense of humanity that has kept our world from coming to an end. The power cut lasted five minutes, but the memory of that incident kept coming back to me again & again. After the meeting, I couldn't help but think about my father's remark.

The light of the torch helped. A light so small helped me find something I had been searching for quite a while. I was able to decipher something that can be helpful to people looking for a positive change in their lives, and I guess that counts us all in.

Science provides us with more outlooks on life and learning than we could ever imagine; how we look at it changes our perspective. It's flabbergasting how a fundamental concept of physics explaining the formation of shadows can teach us so much.

> *"Eyes are always caught by light, but shadows have more to say"*
>
> **– Gregory Maguire**

A shadow is formed on an opaque surface in darkness when there is a light source. The light behind us is what we can't see, and it can be as small as that of a torch but can still help us find what we'd been looking for. Ying and yang, your shadows can give you two views—one showing you who you have become, and one showing who you have become.. The first fosters confidence in your growth, and the second provides insight into your not-so-pleasant side. The darkness in the room will never let you see things through until you let light in.

An opaque surface is just like your willingness to introspect. It's hard, but it's clear and necessary to see your outline. It's challenging to face it sometimes, but it is required to maintain balance in your life, to know when it's green and when it's red. It may or may not be clear, just like mine, but we all have the caliber to figure it out; it's the darkness playing tricks on us, a "shadow's play," as we call it. Never forget that the dark does not destroy the light; it elucidates it.

You can see your shadow alone in a room or out in the open; the choice is yours. Facing your reality can never be harmful; it just takes courage. It breaks myths that we have about us, helping us find the right path to proceed. I know it's all dark outside, but there is always some light we can't see clearly. Reach out to the light because all the beauty in life is made up of shadow and light.

When you are in a dark room, see the light and define your shadow.

HOLE

It is a remarkably compelling creation of nature that concludes anything that ventures into it. A black hole is formed when massive stars collapse under their gravity, and one can only wonder how the object left behind would behave.

Hey there, it's Iris,

I have admired Stephen Hawking for as long as I can remember and have followed his work closely over the years. A BBC interview he gave on black holes caught my eye.

When we view it from a distance, a black hole, or a supernova as some would like to call it, is a dark mass of nothingness and a beautiful work of nature. It's the point of singularity and the end of time. No one knows what's inside a black hole, but we know it's dark black matter with no room for light.

Every natural phenomenon has a message for the living; it tells us something we should know as if the supreme power is trying to connect to you for your good. It's bewitching realizing that we'd known this all this time but couldn't reap what we perceived earlier, and that's precisely what I learned while studying a black hole.

The formation of a black hole symbolizes a toxic human behavior we must be cautious of. The pride of being the best can reduce you to someone who knows nothing because your ego and the sense of being the greatest eventually stops you from learning. When you stop learning, it is when you know nothing.

You will never find a genuinely respected and successful person boasting about their assets and privileges in life. These people will ensure they lead everyday life closely witnessing struggles and learning valuable lessons from everyone they encounter.

Every successful person who isn't drowning in pride has one thing in common, and that is being humble. They understand that no one knows it all, and thus, they have so much to gain. They shine like stars because a great man is always willing to be little.

The stars that collapse under their gravity are like the people who are full of themselves, eventually causing their downfall in life. When these stars collapse, they are entirely ignorant of the light of knowledge and learning because they have an empty void full of darkness that they carry for others.

We must understand that these collapsed stars appear extremely beautiful from a distance, but they are a mass of nothingness inside—empty and hungry to consume you in; these people have no reason to go on because we live to learn.

Remember when you were confident about something, sure that you were better than others, but ruined it for yourself? It's okay to feel that way, but never become that fallen star, because that void will be there to stay.

Knowing nothing is wisdom at the end of the day. So, the next time you think, you know it all,

THINK AGAIN.

DOP-OXY

It was a lovely Sunday afternoon. The child was playing with his dog in their vast backyard, cuddling and laughing, when little Bruno finally learned a new trick. At the same time, his sister stood at least eight feet away, recording a video of them doing the act, and just when they thought she'd join in, she walked away laughing while looking at something on her phone. A week later, talking about that afternoon to their parents, the boy remembered every detail of that episode, smiling as he recounted to his dad how Bruno performed the flips while the big sister looked through her feed to recall what their dog did. She laughed it off. **After all, it was just another day.**

Hey there, it's Iris,

Remember the happiness you felt when, for the first time, the likes in your feeds crossed a century or your follower count increased? That's a dopamine rush. Dopamine is your brain's signal that a reward is at hand. The joyful, excited feeling is released when approaching something that meets an unmet need. It's an instant pleasure but extremely short-lived. The young boy was present with his dog, generating a selfless chemical called Oxytocin. It's a neurochemical of social trust, empathy, understanding, and every emotion that impacts our souls. His elder sister forgot that day, but it remained a beautiful memory for young Fred.

It's better to make memories than to simply get through with days. We are responsible for our lives and what we get out of it; it's incredible how that can be explained through the neurochemical system of our bodies.

In this new age of intimidating social pressure and a constant need for acceptance, almost everyone depends on dopamine to feel happy and fulfilled. Still, in this quest to stay relevant, we often forget that we already have an underrated oxytocin to provide what we are missing in our lives, that constant void we feel.

I'll share a little anecdote: A few years ago, I was a social media addict, seeking acceptance, happiness, and contentment in the likes and comments of people who could vanish from my life the moment I pressed that one button. There were days I used to feel like I was on cloud nine, and the others where I felt devastated and isolated. Little did I know it was the dopamine addiction playing tricks on me, and when I failed to receive that acceptance, drip... drip…drip… in came the cortisol, giving me every bit of anxiety, tension, and stress for pulling me out of the La la Land I created for myself. I had all the happiness in the world, which I was too blind to see. Finally, I gracefully bid farewell to this toxic addiction, making room for oxytocin to work its magic. The feeling you get from this selfless chemical isn't instant, and it takes patience to realize its effects by letting it flow through your veins, but once you do, there is no going back. You become more productive, find time and value for your dear ones because you realize that your life was always here, while you searched for it all over the internet. You find happiness in the slightest of things, and now you have the time to inculcate healthy thoughts in your life. Switching from this selfish to selfless chemical is what it takes.

To put it simply, if infatuation is dopamine, then oxytocin is Love. Both give that rush of happiness; one will leave you before you even know it, and the other is there to stay.

The ride from Dopamine to Oxytocin isn't that hard; all you really need to ask yourself is, **'Where am I Going?'**

CREDENCE

A lion prowled about a field in which Four Oxen used to dwell. He often tried to attack them, but whenever he came near, they turned their tails to one another so that whichever way he approached them, he was met with one of their sharp horns. At last, however, they fell quarrelling among themselves, and each went off to pasture alone in a separate corner of the field. Then the lion attacked them one by one and soon brought an end to all four. – Aesop, sixth century B.C.

What do you think kept them alive?

Hey there, it's Iris,

Undeniably, things we can't see are more accurate, and things we can't hear are more specific. The power of our subconscious mind works mysteriously, as suggested by Joseph Murphy in a beautiful book about how affirming our subconscious and believing in something so firmly that it almost feels genuine can make it happen. That's how the universe works for us; it starts from within. The four oxen were alive because of their faith in themselves as well as others around them, and once they stopped believing in each other, they met their end because nothing on this planet can ever survive without faith.

When we think about faith, it's easy to direct our thoughts toward religious beliefs and customs, but that's not the faith I am talking about; I mean the one that lies inside an atheist, too. The first emotion we experience when we are born is believing that pumping our lungs will help us breathe. This belief can be manifested in both big or small tasks, just like a butterfly has faith that the the flower it sits on will provide nectar, that labor painting a tall bridge has faith that the rope he is tied to will hold him safe, that driver driving the car has faith on the fellow drivers for sticking to their lane and not colliding against him. I had faith over the breakfast I had to fulfill my hunger. This is how the world works; faith drives us in every single day. We live because we believe in others and everything around us.

If somebody tells you that they don't have faith, they are lying to you or to themselves because, in the most practical sense, making decisions about the future, or what we call abductive logic is inevitably influenced by faith-based considerations. Faith is having confidence in what we hope for and assurance about what we see. Believe it or not, you already have faith in yourself; even if it is as small as a mustard seed, you can manifest its power to climb mountains. All it takes is to believe that you can because your credence lies within you.

Shut the voices that tell you that you don't have what it takes. Look inside, and take a leap of faith.

A JUXTAPOSE

I was looking outside, filming every moment of my story—capturing the beauty of life, and the lovely songs. A road trip, how cool and amusing will that be? Everyone is in lockdown, and I feel the fresh air on the highway, with smooth roads and no traffic. Indeed, life is a picnic, a celebration.

Hey there, it's Iris,

Driving the highway a few days ago, I felt elated, and that very moment outside was worth the capture because the source of vitamin D wasn't my pills this time. As I felt the excitement of the road trip and the tune started to set in, I looked across the highway, down to the farms that we often overlook. It started when we stopped for a while; when I clicked a picture of nature's magnificence, my camera caught something I should have seen a long time ago between those beautiful green farms. After zooming in, I saw a lady doing labor in the hot sun, while her two tiny children stood there holding two bags of grains, innocently thinking that those two bags of grains would write their future. This scene was still an aesthetic picture, a #reality of life. I returned to my car, turned on the AC, and insisted on moving.

As we proceeded, I was going through the pictures, and I saw something I hadn't noticed before: the lady's hands were bleeding. She was smiling because her children were looking at her with hope in their eyes—hope that they will have a better life. She didn't want to disappoint them. The children were wearing pretty decent clothes, but that lady was wearing a rugged sari, almost like it was the only one she had. I had goosebumps thinking about the contrast between our lives; what I found beautiful was their way of survival; what I thought would be the perfect post for my story was the reality of their life. It triggered uncomfortable emotions in me when I finally understood a disheartening juxtaposition.

It's chilling to imagine being in their shoes; they go through so much yet still manage to maintain that smile, love, and unity for their family. They understand sacrifice on an entirely different level, which we privileged ones can never know to that extent. What upsets me is that I complained about the long AC and the trip. After this realization struck, my car sped up too fast compared to the villages that crossed by. All I remember was looking around to make the invisible visible to me; I saw men walking on the roads, heading back to their homes, people stuffed in vans and trucks to see their loved ones—while I sat comfortably in a fully equipped car with enough room to stretch my body. How ungrateful we can be was all I could think about.

We have a security of life, but who asks them if they feel secure about themselves or their children? Why is this biased? I know we can't get out of our house today and help them out, but what we *can* do is be grateful for what we have. Feel the gratitude and let that supreme power know you value it.

What I learned from that one picture I accidentally took is that they feel emotions more than we do because they are grounded in the reality and struggles of life. Those struggles don't make them weak but strong enough to give hope they can't even see remotely for their child's happiness. They love beyond what we can understand and give more than we ever could because they know the value of love—what it is like to both give and receive it. Sometimes, they lose track because of the circumstances they are brought into, but we all have a story, don't we? Knowing what you have and being grateful for it will always keep you humble, no matter what you do.

So, the next time you complain about your tea being too sweet. Remember that someone, somewhere, is living on sour milk and still smiling.

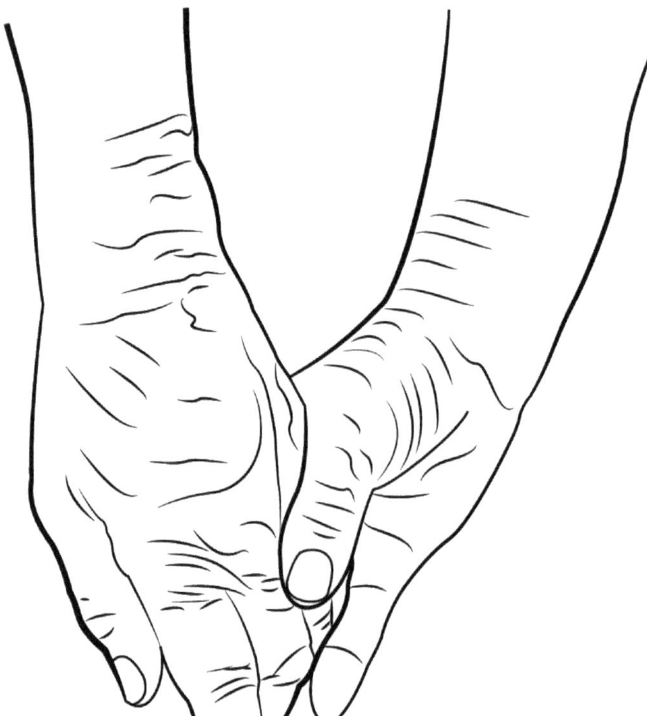

SPECIAL RELATIVITY OF LIFE

A few years ago, I developed a keen interest in time travel after reading a book called *Time Machine* by H.G Wells. Once we start thinking about traveling through time, it tends to capture our hearts and minds, fascinating us with its possibilities. What if we can do it for ourselves?

Hey there, it's Iris,

This isn't science fiction but rather an attempt to help you understand life through a particular relativity theory. So, what is this theory all about? Well, as NASA Quotes in one of its articles on time travel, "Space and time are aspects of the same thing"; time slows down or speeds up depending on how fast you move in relation to something else.

The point I am trying to make here is that regardless of this great piece of work by Albert Einstein, and how luring it sounds, it is practically impossible to travel through time without splitting the atoms of your body, with a 0.01%

chance of flowing through time and coming back in one piece to the time dimension you belong to.

So, my friends, what's DONE IS DONE, but interestingly enough, we all are flowing through time. I have moved a day forward, and so have you. Of course, we can't see time because it's not a visible dimension in our world, but it's there, and we all are traveling through time at a rate of one second per second, or precisely, we are in the present moment at all times.

So, what if we use this time wisely so as to not fall into a state of bitterness later? I strongly believe in connecting the dots and understanding what happened to us by doing so. It's a quiet affirmation that whatever happens, happens for the greater good, but what if I tell you that right now, you have the chance to create a memory that you can either cherish or regret later. The moments in life which we often take for granted, like speaking rudely to our parents for caring too much or fighting with a dear friend, bursting with anger or not offering help to that physically challenged vagabond when we wanted to, just because we were in a hurry for a party or not spending enough time with grandparents and realizing it when it was too late or taking that puff of smoke to look cool when you now suffer from breathing problems or not standing and feeling the grass beneath your shoes completely barefoot, when now you crave to take time out of your busy life to rejuvenate.

This list can go on until we stop taking things for granted and start choosing, speaking, and acting wisely.

I was once going through a short story about a man who asked a wealthy businessman in a conversation at a corporate conference what he regretted most in his life; he told him that he regrets never making it to his son's hockey games and his daughter's dance recitals. That man smiled because even though his net worth was equal to that wealthy man's last paycheck, he made it to everything, and his children always smiled and waved to him during practice and game days.

Much like the relationship between space and time in relativity theory, the time we regret is shaped by the choices we make. The farther we are from how we wish a moment should have been, the more we are stuck in that time, feeling as if it's moving very slowly for us. Keeping it simple, we control all choices in life, so we can either be judicious or worry about them later.

A few years from now, nothing will matter except for our choices and what we could have done differently. **In your hearts, you already know it, don't you?**

Printed by Libri Plureos GmbH in Hamburg,
Germany

9 789367 398524